The Restaurant Planning Guide

The Restaurant Planning Guide
Starting and Managing a Successful Restaurant

Peter Rainsford and David H. Bangs, Jr.

Upstart Publishing Company, Inc.
The Small Business Publishing Company
Dover, New Hampshire

Published by Upstart Publishing Company, Inc.
A Division of Dearborn Publishing Group, Inc.
12 Portland Street
Dover, New Hampshire 03820
(800) 235-8866 or (603) 749-5071

Copyright © 1992 by Peter Rainsford and David H. Bangs, Jr.
All rights reserved. No part of this work may be reproduced or transmitted in any form or by any means without express written consent of the publisher.

Neither the author nor the publisher of this book is engaged in rendering, by the sale of this book, legal, accounting, or other professional services. The reader is encouraged to employ the services of a competent professional in such matters.

Library of Congress Cataloging-in-Publication Data
Rainsford, Peter.
    The restaurant planning guide : starting and managing a successful restaurant / Peter Rainsford and David H. Bangs, Jr.
        p.   cm.
        Includes index.
        ISBN 0-936894-35-0 : $19.95
        1. Restaurant management. I. Bangs, David, H. II. Title.
    TX911.3.M27R35   1992
    647.95'068—dc20   92-27179
                                                                                                  CIP

Printed in the United States of America
10 9 8 7 6 5 4 3 2 1

For a complete catalog of Upstart's small business publications, call (800) 235-8866.

Author's Note

For years I have used Andy Bangs' quote, "A small business is one where you can bring your dog to work." It says so much simply, and it says so much better than the definitions proliferated by various government agencies and academics.

Unfortunately, the saying can't be applied to a restaurant—most health departments would close it down!

Try as I may, I haven't been able to arrive at a simple definition for a restaurant. Perhaps the lack of an easy description is because it is so difficult to be a restaurateur. There are so many factors that come into play, not only is the description difficult, but the task of actually operating a restaurant is extremely complex. My goal with this book is to make the planning for, and the operating of, a restaurant easier. I hope the ideas presented are helpful.

Finally, a heartfelt "thank you" to the thousands of students I have had the privilege of having in the classroom over the years. You have taught me more than I could ever hope to teach you; you have kept me young (at least mentally); and you are the reason that the teaching profession is such a wonderful vocation.

— Peter Rainsford
Ithaca, New York
October, 1992

Table of Contents

Foreword	ix
To the Reader	xi
Introduction	1
Section One: The Business	9
A. Description of Business	10
B. Product/Service	15
C. The Market	17
D. Location of Business	35
E. The Competition	37
F. Management	40
G. Personnel	45
H. Application and Expected Effect of Loan	48
I. Summary	51
Section Two: Financial Data	55
A. Sources and Applications of Funding	59
B. Capital Equipment List	60
C. Balance Sheet	62
D. Break-Even Analysis	67
E. Projected Income Statement	71
F. Cash Flow Projection	81
G. Deviation Analysis	92
H. Historical Financial Reports	101
I. Summary	102
Section Three: The Financing Proposal	105
Section Four: Supporting Documents	113
Appendix One: A Sample Partnership Agreement and Corporate Checklist	117
Appendix Two: Functional Resumes	123
Appendix Three: Resources for Restaurateurs	125
Appendix Four: Glossary	131
Appendix Five: Worksheets	137
Index	157

Foreword

Whether you are thinking about entering the restaurant business, or are already operating a restaurant, *The Restaurant Planning Guide* will be an invaluable addition to your arsenal. *The Restaurant Planning Guide* helps you with the business side of the house. Its clear, direct style and many useful checklists, question sets and forms will make financing, managing and controlling your restaurant much easier. This frees you to enjoy the more creative side of your restaurant—like menu selection, cooking, décor and personal interaction—because you will have the resources that only careful planning and implementation of your plan can bring.

Peter Rainsford, the principal author of *The Restaurant Planning Guide*, brings a lifetime of experience to this book. Peter wears many hats. He is a professor and former assistant dean at Cornell's School of Hotel Administration, the world's premier hospitality academic institution. He is a renowned management consultant who works with restaurants, hotels and hospitality industry suppliers of all kinds. He bales hay. And he owns and manages a restaurant that is oddly similar to Stefanie's Restaurant, the case study used throughout *The Restaurant Planning Guide*.

Peter knows how to *apply* the theoretical strengths of professional restaurant management and knows, from hands-on work in his own restaurant, what works and what doesn't. He knows what questions to ask and when to ask them. He's been a cook. He's waited tables and washed dishes. He's managed bartenders, waitpeople and chefs. He's argued with bankers, wrestled with cash flow problems, and learned when and where to look for professional help. This background makes *The Restaurant Planning Guide* an uncommonly powerful and useful tool.

There are nearly half a million restaurant units in the United States, with an annual turnover rate of 10 to 15 percent each year. A sizeable percentage of the restaurant failures could be avoided by following the planning techniques in *The Restaurant Planning Guide*. Others can become more profitable and more satisfying for their owners and managers. As Peter says, planning is the key to success.

Appendix Three deserves particular notice, not only because it provides information on the National Restaurant Association, but because it will save you a lot of time and effort. There are literally thousands of books and other resources available to help you run your restaurant better. Peter has winnowed the lot and selected the most effective ones for you to use.

That's a good way to think of this book: It *is* effective. *The Restaurant Planning Guide* is designed to help you help yourself. Read it, think about its lessons, follow it—and apply the resulting plan. You'll be glad you did.

— William P. Fisher, PhD
Executive Vice President
National Restaurant Association
Washington, DC

To The Reader

The Restaurant Planning Guide has been developed to help you construct a logically arranged and reasonably complete business plan and financing proposal that will:

- Serve your needs for business analysis;
- Help you design a business plan for your restaurant;
- Provide you with a set of financial forecasts based on your rational assumptions about the future and on your hard-won business experience;
- Set budgeting guidelines—including a working-capital budget and a break-even analysis for your restaurant;
- Help you determine the amount and kinds of financing most appropriate for your restaurant; and
- Give your financing sources the most useful and persuasive information about your restaurant—information they need to make swift, accurate and helpful decisions.

The suggested outline is flexible and you should tailor it to your own needs. It is based on the critical analysis and evaluation of thousands of business plans and financing proposals; on a wide range of resources such as Small Business Administration pamphlets, bank guidelines, textbooks and periodicals; and on conversations with experienced restaurant and business owners, proposal writers, and many readers' comments.

If your plan requires additional information—a time/cost study, for example—include it. If you have trouble understanding how to complete your plan, seek assistance.

A business plan and financing proposal are closely related. In fact, a good business plan that is updated periodically makes the most powerful financing proposal a small business can have. If you follow the guidelines (remembering to adapt them to suit your particular business needs), then you will not only know exactly how much capital you need to make your restaurant work, you will also know and understand what kind of financing to seek and who is most likely to provide it.

This knowledge alone helps you establish credibility with the potential sources of your financing. The complete financing proposal, which is a modification of your finished business plan, will establish maximum credibility. By presenting a clearly thought-out, well-documented financing proposal, you show that you know what you want to do, how to do it, and how the loan will be repaid or the investment will appreciate.

How To Use This Guide

The Restaurant Planning Guide can be used by people contemplating going into the restaurant business as well as those already established in it. There are two major sections in *The Restaurant Planning Guide*, some or all of which will be useful to you depending on your specific needs. The first section is a general discussion of business problems and highlights the main points of the other sections. It is intended to help you identify problem areas and will help you decide which of the other sections will be most useful in problem solving. A glossary defining some of the terminology is included at the end of the book.

The Restaurant Planning Guide is not a substitute for other forms of assistance, but rather points out the need for, and strongly encourages the use of, competent legal, banking and accounting services as well as other specialized forms of assistance.

If at any point in using *The Restaurant Planning Guide* you need further help, seek it out. There are various groups in most areas that provide free or low-cost assistance to small-business owners. Ask your banker about organizations in your area which might be helpful to you.

Each section of the *Restaurant Planning Guide* is divided into three parts:
1. Major points of concern, and why each is important to the success of your restaurant;
2. How to do whatever is required to complete that section;
3. Examples from an actual business plan based on Stefanie's Restaurant. (Stefanie's is a real restaurant that is running profitably under another name.)

When you have finished the process, you will have a complete, coherent document that will serve your needs and the needs of others who may require information from you about your restaurant business.

Requirements for Using This Guide

You must make sufficient time available to do the planning.

This means that you must make the time available. If you are already in business, this may seem impossible. However, while you can hire people to do the work in your restaurant, you cannot hire someone to do the planning for you. The plan is for your business and must be based on your ideas, experience and assumptions. Others can assist you in the process, but you must do the actual planning.

If you are not in business yet but are trying to decide whether your restaurant concept makes sense—or if you have decided and are getting ready to start—following the planning process is the most important thing you can do. It will help you avoid mistakes and save you grief, time and money.

Plan what's going to happen.

Then do it.

Explanation of the Example Used in This Guide

The sample plan that is used throughout *The Restaurant Planning Guide* is based on an actual business plan for a restaurant that was being operated when we finished the book. Dealing with their real-life problems helped to ensure that we were staying on the right track. The planning represented here was accurate and effective. Actual performance turned out to be quite in line with our projections.

Although Stefanie's Restaurant is located in upstate New York, the principles expressed in its planning are universally applicable.

All restaurants, in every part of the country, face the same challenges that Stefanie's faced. Whether you manage a coffee shop, fast-food outlet, or gourmet restaurant, you still must know where you want to go, how you will get there, and what benchmarks are important. You still must work through and with people. You still must use financial controls to manage your business and keep it growing and healthy. Above all, you still must have customers—customers who keep you in business.

About Upstart

Upstart Publishing Company is committed to serving the needs of small businesses everywhere. We can provide a wealth of information to those who are planning to start a business, those who are currently in business, and those who have an interest in and serve small business.

For more information and a free catalog, call us toll free at (800) 235-8866.

Introduction

Why should you go to the trouble of creating a written business plan? There are three major reasons:

1. The process of putting a business plan together, including the thought you put in before beginning to write it, forces you to take an objective, critical, unemotional look at your restaurant project in its entirety.

2. The finished product—your business plan—is an operating tool, which, if properly used, will help you manage your restaurant and work effectively toward its success.

3. The completed business plan communicates your ideas to others and provides the basis for your financing proposal.

The importance of planning cannot be overemphasized. By taking an objective look at your business you can identify areas of weakness and strength, pinpoint needs you might otherwise overlook, spot opportunities early, and begin planning how you can best achieve your business goals. Your business plan also helps you see problems before they grow large and helps you identify their source—thus suggesting ways to solve them. Your business plan will even help you avoid some problems altogether.

This handbook has been designed with these considerations in mind. But you must do the work. A professionally prepared business plan won't do you any good if you don't thoroughly understand it. That level of understanding only comes from being involved from the very start.

Use your plan. Don't put it in the bottom drawer of your desk and forget it. Going into business is rough—over half of all new restaurants fail within the first three years. A major reason for failure is lack of planning. The best way to enhance your chances of success is to plan and follow through on your planning.

Your business plan can help you avoid going into a business venture that is doomed to failure. If your proposed venture is marginal at best, the business plan will show you why and may help you avoid paying the high tuition of learning about business failure. It is far cheaper not to begin an ill-fated business than to learn by experience what a busi-

The best way to enhance your chances of success is to plan and follow through on your planning.

ness plan would have taught you at the cost of several hours of concentrated work.

Finally, your business plan provides the information needed by others to evaluate your venture, especially if you will need to seek outside financing. A thorough business plan can quickly become a complete financing proposal that will meet the requirements of most lenders.

Outline of a Business Plan

- Cover Sheet: Name of business, names of principals, address and phone number
- Statement of Purpose
- Table of Contents

Section One: The Business
    A. Description of Business
    B. Product/Service
    C. Market
    D. Location of Business
    E. Competition
    F. Management
    G. Personnel
    H. Application and Expected Effect of Loan (if needed)
    I. Summary

Section Two: Financial Data
    A. Sources and Applications of Funding
    B. Capital Equipment List
    C. Balance Sheet
    D. Break-Even Analysis
    E. Income Projections (Profit and Loss Statements)
        1. Three-year summary
        2. Detail by month for first year
        3. Detail by quarter for second and third years
        4. Notes of explanation
    F. Cash Flow Projection
        1. Detail by month for first year
        2. Detail by quarter for second and third years
        3. Notes of explanation
    G. Deviation Analysis
    H. Historical Financial Reports for Existing Business
        1. Balance sheets for past three years
        2. Income statements for past three years
        3. Tax returns

Section Three: Supporting Documents
    Personal resumes, personal balance sheets, cost of living budget, credit reports, letters of reference, job descriptions, letters of intent, copies of leases, contracts, legal documents, and anything else relevant to the plan.

The following pages elaborate on and explain each of the above categories.

Introduction

The Cover Sheet

The cover sheet should:

- Identify the business and the document;
- Identify the location and telephone numbers of the business or where the principals can be reached;
- Identify the person who wrote the business plan.

The cover sheet should not be elaborate. It should be neat, attractive and short. If the plan is to be used as a financing proposal, use a separate cover sheet for each bank or capital source you submit it to. See the next page for a suggested cover sheet for a financing proposal.

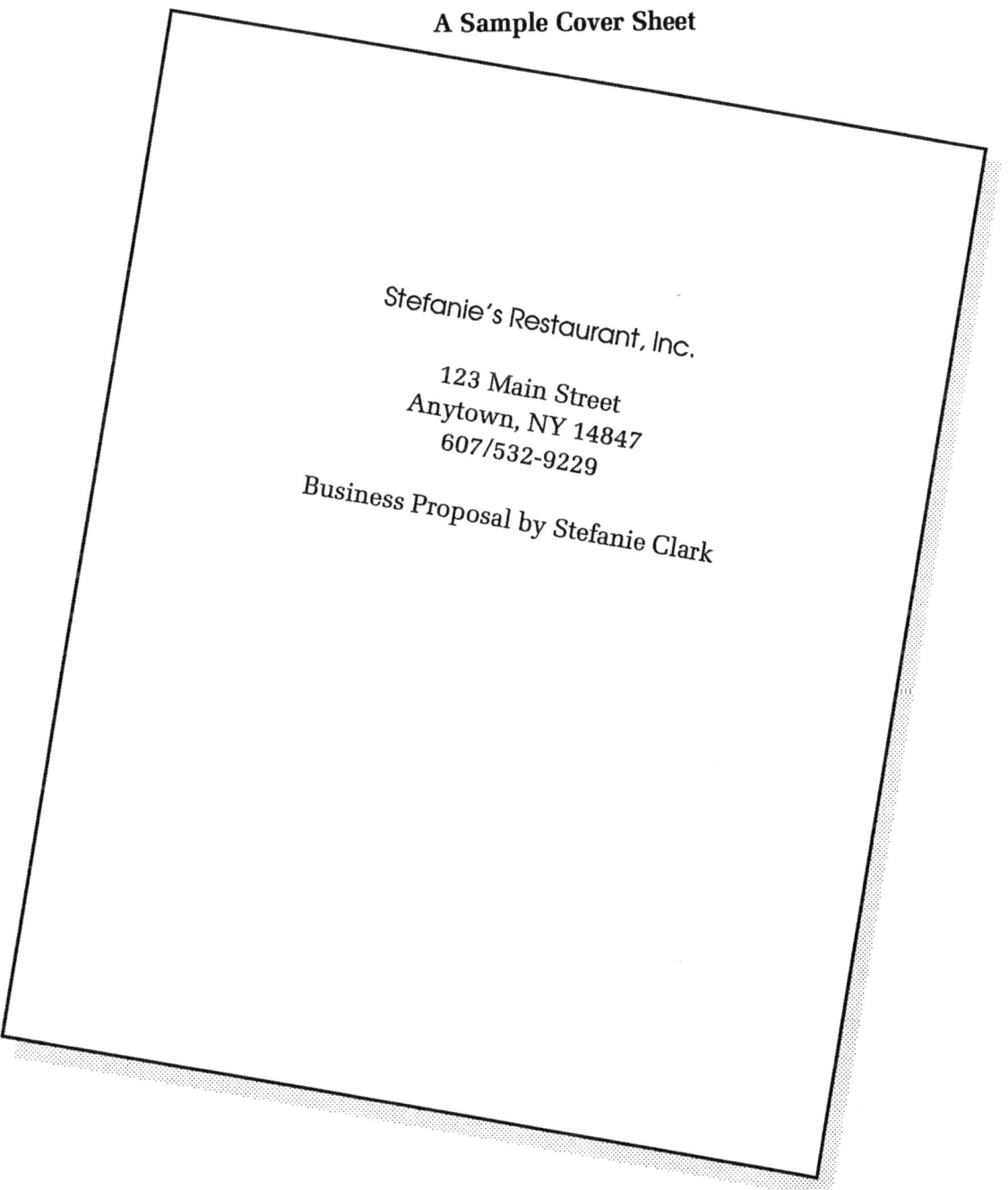

A Sample Cover Sheet

Stefanie's Restaurant, Inc.

123 Main Street
Anytown, NY 14847
607/532-9229

Business Proposal by Stefanie Clark

A Sample Cover Sheet for a Financing Proposal

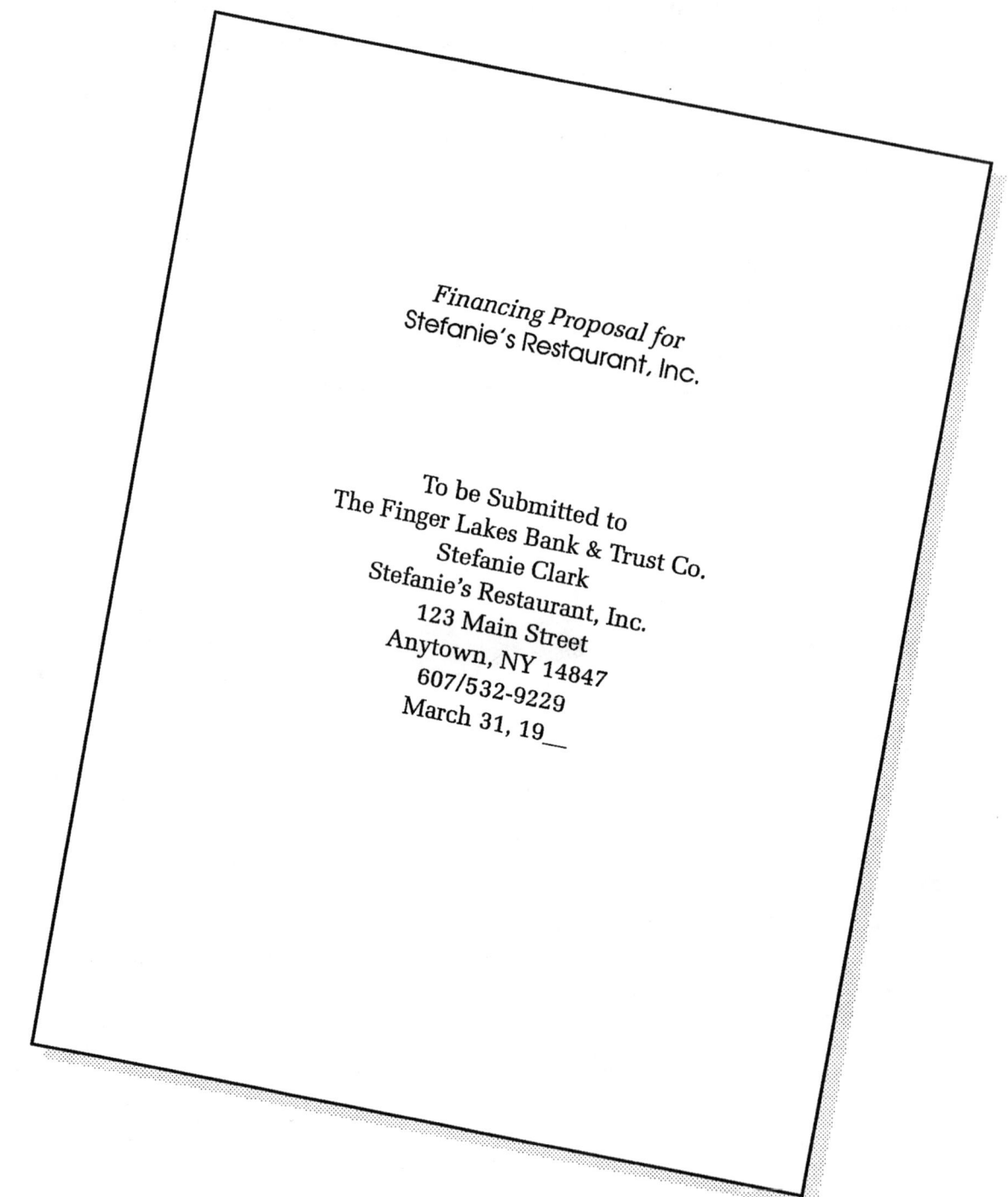

Introduction

Statement of Purpose

The first page of your plan should state your objectives as simply as possible. If the plan is solely for your own use, the statement should be a brief description of how you intend to use the plan once it has been developed. For example: "This plan will be an operating and policy guide for Stefanie's Restaurant, Inc."

If the plan is also to be used as a financing proposal, the statement of purpose becomes more complex. It should include responses to the following questions:

1. Who is asking for money?
2. What is the business structure (for example: sole proprietorship, partnership, corporation, Sub-Chapter S corporation)?
3. How much money is needed?
4. What is the money needed for?
5. How will the funds benefit the business?
6. Why does this loan or investment make business sense?
7. How will the funds be repaid?

The deal you propose—the loan or investment, its use and expected effects on the business, and how you will repay it—will be supported by the rest of your plan. If you are not seeking a loan, the plan should still support and justify the use of your own money (or the money of partners, friends or family).

Keep the statement short and businesslike. It will usually be no longer than half a page, but can be longer if necessary. Use your own judgment.

A Sample Statement of Purpose

Stefanie's Restaurant, Inc. seeks loans totaling $25,000 to: construct an outdoor dining deck; construct additional rest rooms; purchase furniture, fixtures, equipment and inventory; perform necessary renovations and improvements; and maintain sufficient cash reserves to provide adequate working capital to successfully expand an existing lakeside, full-service restaurant. This sum, together with an additional $10,000 equity investment by the principal, will finance transition through the expansion phase so the restaurant can operate at a higher level of profitability.

Notice that this sample statement of purpose contains responses to the checklist items. The last statement is intended to assure the bank that the deal is viable.

The statement of purpose cannot be completed until you have calculated your capital needs. It can be written, but the exact amount needed won't be known until the projections in Section Two: Financial Data have been worked through.

Table of Contents

The Table of Contents should follow your statement of purpose, which is expanded and supported in the remainder of the business plan.

There are three main sections of your plan:

- The Business
- Financial Data
- Supporting Documents

These sections may be broken down further if necessary. Since a business plan, even for a modest deal, can run to 20 or more pages, you want to help the reader find his or her way to sections or subsections of particular interest. The statement of purpose outlines your needs and goals. The table of contents makes it easy to find supporting material.

The table of contents serves as a guide to writing and organizing your business plan.

A Sample Table of Contents

	Page
Section One: The Business	
A. Description of Business	1
B. Product/Service	2
C. Marketing Information	3
D. Location of Business	5
E. Competition	6
F. Management	7
G. Personnel	9
H. Application and Expected Effect of Loan	11
I. Summary	12
Section Two: Financial Data	
A. Sources and Applications of Funding	14
B. Capital Equipment List	15
C. Balance Sheet	16
D. Break-Even Analysis	17
E. Income Projections:	
1. Three-Year Summary	18
2. Detail by Month, First Year	20
3. Detail by Quarter, Second and Third Years	22
4. Notes of Explanation	24
F. Cash Flow Projections	
1. Detail by Month, First Year	26
2. Detail by Quarter, Second and Third Years	28
3. Notes of Explanation	30
Section Three: Supporting Documents	32

A format of this kind makes it easy to find the section of most interest to you at any given time. You will have to fill in the actual page numbers as you go along, but the table of contents serves as a guide to writing and organizing your business plan.

A Brief Note on Financing

Restaurants are considered extremely risky ventures by most commercial lenders, therefore, most of the cash required to start a restaurant is usually provided by the business principals themselves. However, you may need additional funds to launch your business or provide for its growth once it gets started.

Outside funds come in two forms: equity or debt.

Equity funds come from selling a portion of the business to yourself or another person. The amount you have to sell to acquire the needed funds reflects the amount of risk that the investor perceives. If your venture seems very risky, you may have to sell a substantial share. If it is not seen as very risky, you won't have to give up as much ownership. Hence, it is greatly to your advantage to make the perceived risk as low as possible—and a business plan can do this.

Debt is a loan, usually from a bank, that the lender expects you to repay at some determinate time. The lender will ordinarily want to receive a return for the use of the funds in the form of interest. The interest rate reflects the lender's perceived risk. The higher the perceived risk, the higher the rate. Your plan must take into account the need to repay both principal and interest as agreed. This has far-reaching effects on your profits and cash flow, so borrow with care.

If you use an outside equity investor, you don't have to repay the funds, but you give up a share of ownership and will have to share decision making and profits. If the business grows to the point where you wish to sell out, the real cost of an equity investor can be far greater than interest on a loan.

If you use bank debt, you may find yourself subject to loan agreements that effectively compel you to share decision making with your creditors. For example, an agreement may limit the amount of debt you can incur relative to the net worth of the business, which can force you to find new equity money in order to grow.

You will find that more advice on these kinds of concerns will be very helpful. Your banker or accountant can provide this advice (and in any case you should be in close communication with both your banker and your accountant as you plan your business).

A brief discussion of different types and sources of financing is included at the end of this book—see page 109.

It is greatly to your advantage to make the perceived risk as low as possible—and a business plan can do this.

Section One: The Business

This is the most important and most difficult part of your business plan. The objective of this section is to make a clear statement of:

1. What the business is (or will be);
2. What products and/or services you plan to offer;
3. What markets you intend to service, the size of those markets and your expected share;
4. How you can service those markets better than your competition;
5. Why you have chosen your particular location;
6. What management and other personnel are available and required for the operation; and
7. Why (if appropriate) debt money or someone's equity investment will make your business more profitable.

These seven statements are crucial. Together they will form the written policy of your business, rules you shouldn't deviate from without compelling reasons. Policy establishes direction and lends stability to your business. Direction and stability are as important to a business as to a tightrope walker—so give them a great deal of thought and planning.

In describing your business idea, otherwise known as your mission statement, aim for clarity and simplicity. A rule of thumb: If you can't describe your idea clearly and simply, you haven't thought it through.

Remember that the technical support for your business idea will be found primarily in the Financial Data and the Supporting Documents sections. In the Business section, refer to the supporting information as needed. Too much detail gets in the way of explaining your idea.

A rule of thumb: If you can't describe your idea clearly and simply, you haven't thought it through.

A. Description of Business

The objective of this section is to explain:

- What your business is;
- How you are going to run it; and
- Why you think your business will succeed.

Your entire planning effort is based on your perception of what business you are in.

Deciding the type of restaurant and its market focus are the most important decisions you have to make.

Any restaurant can be involved in more than one activity. If so, your judgment of what the central activity is (or what the central activities are) is crucial. Your entire planning effort is based on your perception of what type of restaurant business you are in. If you make a serious error at this point, your chances of success will be sharply diminished. So be sure to think this decision through.

The Description of Business section answers these seven basic questions:

1. What business are you in? Is your restaurant counter, table service, or take-out? Is your restaurant fast-food, full-service, or gourmet? What is your menu? Who are your customers?

2. What is the status of the business: A start-up? An expansion of a going concern? A takeover of an existing restaurant? A division of a larger restaurant chain? A franchise?

3. What is the business's form: sole proprietorship, partnership, corporation? (Your attorney's advice is essential if you are starting up a business. Use the sample partnership agreement and corporate checklist in Appendix One as a guideline. Since the legal and tax implications are so complex, you need your attorney's and accountant's advice.)

4. Why is your restaurant going to be profitable (or continue to grow)?

5. When will (did) your restaurant open?

6. What hours of the day and days of the week will you be (are you) in operation?

7. Is your restaurant seasonal? If it is or if the hours will be adjusted seasonally, make sure the seasonality is shown in your replies to five and six.

The first question is the toughest to answer concisely, since it is the linchpin of your plan and it involves the questions mentioned above. It certainly calls for more detail than a simple, "Stefanie's Restaurant will serve the finest kind of food at the lowest possible prices" kind of statement. (See page 14 for a more detailed example.)

Section One: The Business

Knowing exactly what your business does and how it operates enables you to effectively plan for profits. This means you must be able to clearly identify the goals of your business at the beginning of your planning. Once the goals are clear, then you can start figuring out ways to make a profit. As the business progresses, the question of how to make profits must be continuously asked and answered. (Making profits is what business is about. Even nonprofit organizations must have revenues that exceed expenses to survive.)

Focus is the aim. The tighter your focus, the less time and money you'll waste. If you know what business you are really in, you'll concentrate your efforts and use your resources efficiently.

Attention to profit planning will help you identify what is special about your restaurant and why it won't be one of the 50 percent or more that disappear before their second anniversary.

You will not yet have a complete answer to question four since it will be partially answered in the financial projections in Section Two: Financial Data. Keep in mind that the answers will come out as your business plan progresses.

Questions five, six and seven are particularly important for restaurants. These are marketing and staffing questions that will be addressed later in the plan.

Since start-ups and takeovers face different kinds of problems, they are treated separately on the following pages. The following checklists supplement questions one through seven.

For a New Restaurant

Your Description of Business section should be based on responses to the following questions (as well as the basic seven). These questions will come up again and again—and as your restaurant grows, your answers will change.

    1. Why will you succeed in this restaurant?
    2. What is your experience in the restaurant business? Lack of experience is one of the leading causes of business failure. But fortunately, it's a risk you can avoid. Before you launch your own restaurant, gain experience and learn the ins and outs of your proposed business by working for someone else. Ideally, you would work in management for at least a year. All businesses are more complex when seen from within than when viewed from the outside.
    The owner of Stefanie's Restaurant had the necessary experience before she opened the business, having previously worked in several restaurants and graduated from a four-year college with a major in restaurant management.

Take advantage of possible insights and experience of competitors.

3. **Have you spoken with other people in this kind of restaurant business? What did you learn from them?**

4. **What will be special about your restaurant?** Restaurants are competitive—and standing out from the competition is increasingly important. Many restaurant owners fail to take advantage of possible insights and experience of competitiors. They are your best single source of information and will often give you valuable advice for nothing more than a chance to show their expertise. Talking with them (and observing their business practices) will also help you define what the special advantages of your own business will be.

5. **Have you spoken with prospective trade suppliers to find out what managerial and/or technical help they will provide?**

6. **Have you asked about trade credit?** Trade credit is a source of funds. Terms such as "2/10, net 30" allow you to use the supplier's money for the 30 days—it's like a non-interest bearing loan for that period. However, this also means that you forego the cash discount allowed for payment within ten days. Taking discounts can represent a substantial savings on the cost of the product: By paying within ten days, you save two percent of net. This cash discount represents an annualized rate of 36 percent. (Saving two percent by paying 20 days sooner is the same as earning two percent for a 20-day period—and there are 18 such periods each year.) If you can borrow funds somewhere else for less interest, you should take advantage of the savings.

Trade credit is often not available until a business has been in operation long enough to establish a reputation for paying on time.

Many suppliers offer free services as an inducement to buy their product. For instance, restaurant equipment suppliers provide free layout advice; utility companies give hints on how effective use of lighting can create more sales; carbonated beverage suppliers provide free dispensing systems.

7. **How will you offset the slow payment of your customers?** Most restaurant sales are either cash or credit card, but if you intend to promote house accounts for either individuals or companies, you should be concerned with credit terms.

For a Takeover

Your Description of Business should contain a brief history of the restaurant you plan to take over and provide answers to the following questions.

Make sure you can answer these thoroughly. Your banker and other investors will want detailed information. If you don't have these answers, chances are you won't get the financing.

1. **When and by whom was the business founded?**
2. **Why is the owner selling it?**
3. **How did you arrive at a purchase price for the restaurant?** Restaurants that are strong and growing are rarely offered for sale, and

Section One: The Business

most sellers will give (not necessarily deliberately) misleading reasons for selling their business.

Protect yourself. Ask your banker to check out the business. This is a common procedure, since bankers can get information you may not have access to. If your lawyer and accountant have had a lot of experience buying and selling businesses, get their advice. (They will be involved anyway. Buying a restaurant is a major financial commitment, and you will want all the help you can get.)

A strong case can be made that buying a going restaurant with a positive cash flow is a lot less risky than starting a restaurant from scratch. You might want to contact a professional restaurant broker to help you find the right restaurant, or provide you with an updated listing of restaurants you might be interested in buying.

Pricing a business—especially a small or closely held company that is not publicly traded—is a delicate and demanding process. It calls for both expertise and ethics. Paying for a professional appraisal may turn out to be an excellent investment, as it not only establishes a fair price for the restaurant but also provides justification for the price should outside financing be needed.

Pricing a business calls for both expertise and ethics.

Include a copy of the appraisal as a document supporting the price. The price should reflect the value of the assets of the business, the rate of expected return on your investment (including new investment in the business during the first few years), and some "going concern" or goodwill figure.

Since you will be repaying the purchase price out of profits, make sure that you get what you pay for. Be careful—and seek professional help.

4. What is the trend of sales?

5. If the restaurant profits are going downhill, why? How can you turn them around?

Questions four and five should be supported by income statements and tax returns. Remember, if a business is sliding downhill, there may be reasons that aren't immediately apparent. Check out the owner's reasons for selling. Ask his or her bankers. It is difficult to restore a tarnished reputation, and it can't be done overnight.

6. How will your management make the business more profitable? If you can turn around a faltering business, the rewards can be great. Just make sure that you have the skills, capital, and patience turnarounds require before you commit yourself.

As you check out the business, always remember to:

- Evaluate and determine a value for perishable and non-perishable inventory.
- Evaluate and verify the china, silver and glassware inventories.
- Check with trade creditors.
- Determine the age of the receivables.
- Determine the age and condition of the kitchen equipment and physical plant.

- See if the business owes money. (If it does, will you inherit the liabilities?)
- See if there are any legal problems pending.

You are planning to put your money on the line. Don't be afraid to ask for advice before you commit yourself to any deal. A good attorney and accountant are essential at this point to make sure the transaction benefits both sides—especially if seller financing will be involved, as is usually the case.

A Sample Description of Business
Stefanie's Restaurant, Inc. is a full-menu, table service, casual restaurant. It is of log cabin construction and is one of only two restaurants on Lake Delaney with docking facilities for boaters. At present, about 60 percent of sales occur in the summer months, and business is turned away during that time period. Stefanie's Restaurant plans to increase its capacity during the heavy demand summer tourist and boating season and to target individuals and small groups during the remaining months of the year. Stefanie's Restaurant began business in March, 19__. The restaurant is open seven days a week for lunch and dinner during the summer season from noon until 10:00 P.M. During the remainder of the year, the restaurant is closed on Mondays and Tuesdays. The demand is seasonal and fluctuates according to the weather. The restaurant is currently forced to turn away patrons during the summer tourist season—especially when the weather is conducive to arrival by boat. In order to accommodate this excess demand, Stefanie's Restaurant proposes to construct a dining deck, which will increase the capacity during the busy season, but will not place excess demands on the business during the off-season. Since Stefanie's already has a reputation for quality freshly prepared food at competitive prices, efforts will be made to attract patrons back in the winter months by direct marketing techniques and the development and promotion of group business functions for up to 80 people.

Note that this description answers most of the questions posed on the various checklists on pages 10 through 13. (But remember that the checklists are meant to provide a guideline, not a straitjacket.)

It should be apparent that Stefanie's Restaurant has a well-defined marketing strategy. They will be expanding their capacity during the heavy demand season and targeting individuals and groups for business in the slow season. The dining deck will allow Stefanie's to expand with a minimal investment, yet will not create a facility that needs to be maintained during the slow winter months.

This is a careful strategic move. They think they see a way to develop a competitive advantage in the summer market niche, based on their experience and lack of competition, by expanding capacity.

Section One: The Business

B. Product/Service

Most restaurants are built around products and/or services that already are available. A restaurant such as Stefanie's has a very simply described menu; the service element involves how they prepare the product and serve the food to their customers.

If your menu or service location is unique or otherwise noteworthy, take advantage of it. Such differentiation is valuable, tends to be fleeting, and attracts imitators.

The products and/or services offered by most businesses are generic. While you may believe your products and services are special, that perception is not necessarily shared by your market, and no amount of advertising is apt to change their perception. A hardware store sells hardware; a lawyer sells legal services; a restaurant sells food.

Differentiating your foods and service from those of the competition starts with thorough product or service knowledge. One of the most important aspects of restaurant management is giving your markets reasons to patronize your restaurant—and one of the best reasons is that the benefits you offer meet the market's desires. People tend to buy what they want, not what you think you offer.

Even if you mention your menu and service only in passing in your business plan, you should go through the exercises below. They will help you understand better how to position your restaurant—and can make a difference when your banker asks what's so special about your restaurant.

The key question is not: "What are your products or services," but rather:

1. What are you selling? You may think you're selling hardware in your hardware store, that is, hammers and saws and nails and buckets of paint. Your customers, on the other hand, think they're buying (along with the hammers, saws, nails and paint) savings, improved homes, fulfillment of a do-it-yourself ethic—and they choose your hardware store because it's convenient, clean, staffed with polite clerks, has good parking, and so on.

Give your markets reasons to buy your products.

The same applies to a lawyer. People seldom buy legal advice, they buy solutions to legal problems, a sympathetic ear, a champion of their cause, peace of mind, and so on.

Stefanie's Restaurant sells good service, a view of the lake, accessibility by boat, a pleasant excursion getting there (by boat or by a scenic drive along the lakeshore) along with the freshly prepared food they thought they were selling.

2. What are the benefits (as opposed to the features) of what you are selling?

3. How does your restaurant differ from the competition? Customers buy benefits. Features make those benefits possible—the freshness of Stefanie's Restaurant's foods are features; the taste and the implications of fresh, natural, healthy foods are among the benefits customers perceive. Other restaurants offer other benefits—more convenient locations, proven reputation (habit is powerful), lower prices. Stefanie's can't compete on every front; they hope to dominate one niche of the restaurant business in a local market by a strategy of product differentiation.

4. If your menu items are new or not well established in your geographical area, what makes them different? Desirable? Educating a market to a new product is fraught with danger and unexpectedly high costs.

5. If your product or service line is not special, why would people buy from you? Convenience? A wide product line? Price? Service?

Business success comes from satisfying market needs. In only a few businesses does that edge come from product superiority or high tech. Most business—whether retail, wholesale, or service—is pretty mundane.

Don't rely on your "superior" product or service. Do rely on satisfying your market's needs. The first step toward this goal is to understand all about your product and service: What are their features? What benefits can they provide the customer? How can you use your product or service knowledge to differentiate your restaurant from competing restaurants?

The second, more important step comes in the next section of the business plan: What do your customers want?

Section One: The Business

C. The Market

Two important maxims to keep in mind throughout this section are:

1. Minimize opportunities for customer dissatisfaction; and
2. Marketing wars are never won—they are always lost.

In this section you will develop a marketing strategy, a plan within a plan. You want to make sure you don't lose the marketing war by making avoidable mistakes. Your restaurant succeeds or fails according to how well you satisfy your market's perceptions, wants and expectations. This means that you have no option but to learn who your customers and prospects are, why they patronize your restaurant or someone else's, and what you can do about getting more customers.

You must be thoroughly knowledgeable about your market, the people who patronize or will patronize your restaurant. You need a stream of customers who will buy your goods and service, at a price that yields a profit, over a sufficient period to keep your restaurant healthy and growing.

There are four basic marketing moves:
1. Sell old products to old customers. This is the least risky strategy.
2. Sell new products to old customers.
3. Sell old products to new customers.
4. Sell new products to new customers. This is the most risky strategy.

Your first challenge is: Define your target markets.

Your first challenge is: Define your target markets.

Start with your current customers. They find what you offer them to be of value. If you are in a start-up restaurant, who do you think your customers will be? Your aim is to know in detail what your customers want that your restaurant can profitably provide.

Marketing has the customer as its sole focus. Everything in your restaurant, whether it's a start-up or a going concern, old or new, big or small, revolves around your customers and the people you want to have as customers. Your menu and service have to be tailored to their perceptions of what is worth buying. Your location and hours of operation have to fit their needs. Management and staff have to be selected and trained with one goal in mind: satisfying your customers and keeping them coming back. Even the capital structure of the business revolves around the customer. If you can persuade your bankers, investors, and suppliers that you have a strong and stable customer base, you won't lack capital.

It sounds so simple: Put the customer first and the profits will follow. In practice, of course, it's far more difficult.

Your marketing plan gives you a way to define, understand and satisfy your target markets. Write it down. It involves too many variables and is too important to be left to chance.

Three Parts to the Business Plan

1. **Concept**
   - What kind of restaurant business are you in?
   - Why is it the right business for you to be in?
   - What would you like your restaurant to be famous for?
   - What do you sell?
   - Why will people patronize your restaurant?
   - Who are your competitors?
   - How can you stand out in the crowded restaurant market?

2. **Customers**
   - Who are (and will be) your customers?
   - What benefits do you (can you) provide them?
   - How many of them are there?
   - How many customers do you need?
   - What are their buying patterns?
   - What restaurants do they currently go to?
   - How will they know about your restaurant?

3. **Capital (or Cash)**
   - How much capital do you need?
   - How can you maintain cash flow and liquidity?
   - How much working capital do you need?
   - What kind of budgets should you follow?
   - How can you control your finances?
   - How much growth can you afford—and how much do you want?

Marketing is the process of creating and retaining customers. Your strategic marketing plan is built on realistic answers to three basic questions:

1. What kind of restaurant business are you in? Look at your mission statement again. Your mission statement helps you position your restaurant in the marketplace. What makes your restaurant unique? The concept of positioning is critical to your promotional and advertising efforts and will be considered below. What do you want your restaurant to become?

2. Who are your target markets? Who is your ideal customer? You can't serve everyone. There used to be a store near Keene, New Hampshire, that proudly boasted, "We have Everything for Everybody!" Not even the largest international corporation can claim everyone as its prospect. The focus implied by "target marketing" carries

Section One: The Business

over into finding ways to limit your markets because you have only so many hours and so many dollars to find and satisfy your customers and prospects.

3. What benefits do your customers think they receive from your menu and service?

Providing informed answers to these questions is difficult. Marketing is a mixture of art (in the guise of your hunches and experience, insights and vision) and science (in the form of careful research and attention to facts). If marketing were simple, no business would ever fail. Your marketing plan helps you make sure that you keep all the pieces of the marketing puzzle in balance.

What goes into a marketing plan? There are at least eight pieces. While they will be presented here as if they come one after another, in the real world they are so interrelated that you can't separate them. As a simple example, your pricing decision will be driven by how your markets perceive the benefits they gain from what you offer them. Their perceptions are influenced by (and will influence) your positioning and promotional efforts, which you adopt at least in part in response to what your competition is up to. And this is just the beginning.

Don't be daunted. You can start anywhere. The following descriptions and question lists are intended to stimulate your thinking. For an indepth look at marketing, see *The Market Planning Guide* by David H. Bangs, Jr.

I. Customers

This is where your market planning begins. Customer focus is the crux of your marketing efforts. There is no substitute for thoroughly understanding your markets. Start with the customers you currently have. The questions you must be able to answer include:

1. **What are your markets?**
2. **Which ones are buying from you now?**
3. **What products/services are they buying?**
4. **Who are the people that are buying from you?**

These are base-line questions. It's easy to broadly characterize markets you now serve. Stefanie's Restaurant has at least three: summer tourists, boaters, and local residents who drive to the restaurant. These constitute current markets, and their purchasing habits can be fairly readily ascertained by observation and some sampling. Determining a market's characteristics is a favorite task for business school classes—and can cost you as little as the out-of-pocket costs for the students and their professor.

The simplest demographic segmentation of your target markets will vault you ahead of most of your competitors, who rely on habit and inertia rather than analysis of their markets. "Demographic seg-

Customer focus is the crux of your marketing efforts.

mentation" is a marketing analysis that targets groups of prospects by factors such as sex, age, marital status, income, occupation, life style, family size, and education.

If you have customers already, start with them. See who patronizes your competition. Carefully study trade journals, the more specific to your business the better. Call up the editors of restaurant trade magazines—market studies, including customer profiles and other useful information, are stock in trade for these experts, and they will be glad to steer you to more information. These indirect sources of customer information are especially useful for start-up restaurants.

You want to be able to identify the best (most profitable to you) prospects and understand them well enough to be able to satisfy their perceived needs.

5. How would you characterize your markets? Some market segmentation criteria that might help are listed below. These are suggested as starting points only. Your markets will have criteria specific to them.

Why is this so important? Segmentation of your markets provides the basis for all subsequent marketing and promotional efforts. If you know who your best prospects are, then you can find out what they want and use their point of view to guide all of your restaurant's activities. There is no other way to put the customer first.

If you do not know who your customers are (or will be), there is no way to find out what they want. You can't advertise effectively; you can't develop menus or services that meet their desires; you can't get ahead of your competitors. What you can do—if you think you know it all already and don't have to go to the effort of analyzing and understanding your markets—is trust to dumb luck and and correct your inevitable blunders by following behind the market leader, thus relegating your restaurant to (at best) an also-ran position.

Sample demographic segmentation criteria:
For individuals:
- Age
- Gender
- Race and ethnic group
- Hobbies
- Life style
- Reading, listening and viewing patterns (newspapers, magazines, TV, radio)
- Education
- Social class
- Occupation
- Income level
- Family life cycle

For group business:
- Type of functions
- Size of functions

- Special requirements
- Menu needs

Segmenting and categorizing your customers and prospects makes sense for even the smallest restaurant. It is a necessity for a new restaurant, one in transition, or a business in a rapidly changing market where an experienced "feel" for the customer base is lacking or no longer applies. That feeling is a poor substitute for segmentation, but it is better than nothing. Augmented by segmentation analysis, your sense of who the market consists of becomes a powerful competitive weapon.

II. Product Benefits

As noted above in Section B: Product/Service, customers don't buy products or services, they buy benefits. The benefits they perceive are very often not those that you might have spotted, which is why surveys and other methods to find out what your customer wants are so important.

Customers don't buy products or services, they buy benefits.

"What's in it for me?" is the question every customer implicitly asks. They may not express it in this way, but they all want to know, "If I go to this restaurant, what do I gain?" Your prospects have wants and needs and they see a variety of ways to meet them. If you manage to present your menu and service in such a way to convince customers that your restaurant is the best—the fastest, most economical or enjoyable—you'll get their business. This, by the way, is one way to define positioning (see below for more information).

This knowledge does not come from sitting back in an armchair and theorizing about what your customers might want—or worse, should want. Buying behavior is just not that rational. It's one of those areas where guesses don't pay off but research does.

The simplest research? Just go to your customers and ask what they do and do not like about your restaurant, menu, service, sales methods and so on. People like to have their opinion solicited.

You want answers to the following questions:

1. Why do these people come to my restaurant?
2. Why do they patronize us and not the competition?

Unless you know who your customers, prospects and competition are, you can't even begin to ask these questions. You can get help with marketing surveys from small-business development centers, small-business institutes, marketing courses at local business schools, and from your trade association. Surveys can be tricky. Customers don't always give straight answers to direct questions, and interpreting the data can be a challenge, so use whatever help you can get.

You will be surprised at what surveys turn up. Customers buy from you because your location is convenient, or your waitpeople are polite and well-informed, or because they think your competitors are arrogant, rude, brusque and disdainful. Your service may or may not be perceived to be superior; your menu may or may not be price competitive. But there will be reasons why you get their trade and your competitors do not. On the other hand, when you lose customers to the competition you want to know what you are doing wrong—or what competitive restaurants are doing better than you.

3. What do they buy from us? On what cycle?

There are two levels to question three. On the surface, customers buy the things you sell them—food and beverages.

Service businesses, including restaurants, have some non-tangible inventories, which present a special problem. A hotel room is either booked for the night or not; a restaurant table is occupied or not. You have to manage your inventories carefully, and this comes from knowing when people are most apt to patronize your restaurant. The buying cycle of your customers affects your scheduling. All restaurants have such cycles. The cycles may be subtle, but your customers buy your goods and services in patterns that you can understand if you make the effort to observe them.

The second level is concerned with perceived benefits. You have to look at what you sell through the eyes of your customers and prospects. People buy benefits, the gains or rewards they expect to receive from your products. This is always complex. Max Factor, the cosmetics king, said, "Our factories make cosmetics. We sell hope." The things sold (lipstick, perfume, eye shadow, mascara and so forth) have physical characteristics or features such as color, weight, fragrance and texture. The customer couldn't care less about these physical characteristics. She is buying hope—hope for approval, hope for beauty, hope for a new mate or retaining the old one and so forth. Features are only important insofar as they convey benefits to the prospective buyer.

By focusing on the perceived benefits (the "what's in it for me?") you make positioning your restaurant much simpler. You may be selling fresh seafood and asparagus, but your customers are buying health and pleasant surroundings and freedom from washing dishes at home. And so on.

The key question: What features of your menu and service convey benefits to the customer? How does your customer perceive your offerings? What are the benefits you ultimately provide that customer?

Don't beat this into the ground. Use common sense. Place yourself in your customer's shoes. Ask questions. Listen to the responses. Once you know what benefits your restaurant should provide, provide them. Your restaurant will flourish.

4. How can we find more people like these?

Question four drives your future strategies. It is always easier to sell to current customers than to new ones, but you have to constantly

The key question: What features of your menu and service convey benefits to the customer?

look for more customers to replace those you lose through normal attrition and to competitors, to say nothing of the new customers you need in order to grow more profitable.

People cluster by interests and expectations. Once you know what people are buying, why they buy from you, and who those people are (by description as well as direct personal acquaintance), you can find more people like them.

III. Sales and Distribution

The challenge is to deliver your goods and services to the customer economically. Part of this is a function of your location. A good location (see Section D: Location) makes it easy for customers to find you, and makes it possible for you to serve those customers in a favorable way. The other part is concerned with sales practices, how you help the customer meet his or her needs. While that subject is well beyond the scope of this book, the idea behind strategic sales efforts is simple: make it easy for your customer to buy from you by providing services like an in-state 800 number for reservations, charge accounts and accepting credit cards.

A Brief Note on Credit

Offering credit costs you money. It can have a negative effect on your cash flow, especially in the early stages. You may have to borrow money for working capital to carry customer credit. You may strangle your business by tying up funds you could have used more profitably elsewhere.

The restaurant business is generally considered a "cash business" since most customers expect to pay for their meals at the time of purchase. Even credit card sales are considered "cash" since payment is guaranteed if the company is called for a verification number. You may, however, extend credit if you establish house accounts for area businesses or individuals. Such house accounts may provide you with a competitive advantage over your competition. You will also need to establish and clearly define good credit policies if you cater large functions. After serving a banquet of 200 people, you have little recourse when the individual booking the function tells you they can't pay. The food cannot be returned and the staff must be paid!

Being a "cash business" also has several special problems that you must pay careful attention to. The large amounts of cash can be easily accessible to many people, both employees and customers. Be certain that you develop proper controls to minimize any possibility of theft, not only of cash, but also of food and beverages.

IV. Competition

Who are your competitors? You can learn a lot from them: What do they do better than you? Less well than you? How do they please their customers? What is their pricing policy? Where and how do they advertise, and does it work?

Your suppliers will have insights into what your competition is doing and what people in similar restaurants in non competitive areas (another city or state) are doing. If you feel bold enough (or are in a start-up or transitional restaurant) take a trip and visit restaurants like yours. Restaurant owners love to talk about their restaurants if (a) they aren't talking to direct competitors, (b) you make an appointment at their convenience, and (c) you let them know beforehand what you are going to ask.

Information is power. Most restaurant owners do not take the time to painstakingly assemble competitive information. There is nothing wrong or immoral about scouting the competition—athletes and armies do it all the time. So should you. This will give you a strong competitive edge.

V. Positioning, Publicity and Promotion

In *Ogilvy on Advertising*, David Ogilvy, founder of a hugely successful advertising firm, wrote that of the thirty-two things his advertising company had learned, the most important was positioning. Positioning is a marketing method in which you determine what market niche your restaurant should fill, and how it should promote its products or services in light of competitive and other forces.

The importance of establishing a market niche is hard to overstate.

Positioning is important for all businesses, but especially for small businesses that lack the depth of resources to weather a major marketing blunder. The importance of establishing a market niche is hard to overstate. Pick a market big enough to support you and allow you to grow your restaurant, yet tight enough to defend against competitors. You simply cannot afford to market too broadly. The economics are overwhelming.

Your recourse is positioning. Pick a niche in which you can become a presence. This can be as simple as locating your restaurant where there is little competition, keeping hours that suit the convenience of your customers, and stocking the foods and beverages they want. The idea is to differentiate your restaurant from competing restaurants, which means you must know what they are up to (hence the study of the competition) and who your customers are and what they want that other restaurants aren't providing.

A market niche is much like a target market except (in most cases) a little more tightly defined in terms of how you can reach that market. Stefanie's advertises in local newspapers, on local radio, posts flyers at marinas and at launching ramps, utilizes direct mail, and uses their location and signage to reach local markets. They zero in on their target markets, using the proverbial rifle rather than a shotgun approach.

Aiming promotions at targeted markets is the safest way to stretch your promotional dollars and gain market share. By this point you should be able to decide what image and message you want to project.

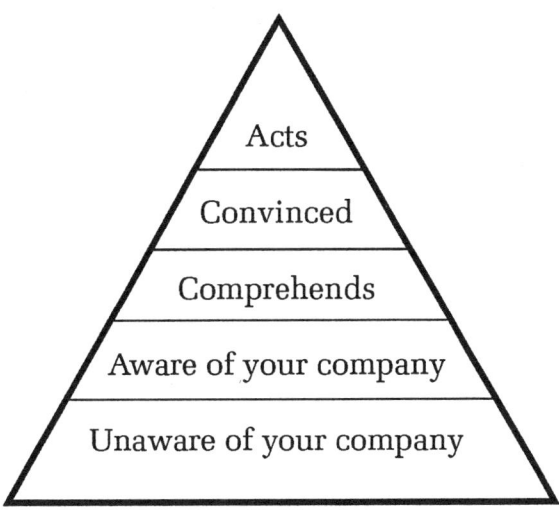

The Promotion Pyramid

What will make your customers and prospects think of your restaurant when they want to dine out?

Promotion and Advertising Note
Since you know who your prospects are (the target market in your market niche) you can determine where your prospects are on the Promotion Pyramid. The notion behind the pyramid is that you can move people along one step at a time. If they don't know that you're in business, let them know. If they know you have a restaurant, what does it take to persuade them that you are going to be able to meet their needs? What will it take to get them to act? Do they understand what you want to sell them, or will you have to educate them first?

Stefanie's has been around for over a year now, so local residents know where the restaurant is and what's appealing about it: Who they are, the quality and service they offer, the special magic of Stefanie's Restaurant's location and so on. Therefore, Stefanie's can advertise specials: "New Improved Fran's Special!" or "Fresh lobster!" or whatever they think would move their market to act.

As you figure out how to promote your restaurant using all the tools available to you, including public relations and advertising, there are three myths to avoid. If you are already in the restaurant business you probably know these; if you are new to business, they are hazardous to your economic well being.

The first myth is, "You can rely on 'word-of-mouth' advertising." This is usually an excuse not to invest in advertising rather than a good way to gain customers. Passive word-of-mouth is always ineffective. Happy customers tell an average of 0.7 other people if they have had a positive experience with you. Unhappy customers tell 7 to 11 other people! That is why minimizing opportunities for customer dissatisfaction is so important. Word-of-mouth advertising can be made to work, but it requires discipline and a programmatic effort. Ask customers for referrals. Make it easy for them—give them brochures, flyers, samples or whatever it takes to make your case. Then follow up.

The second myth is that only highly creative and clever advertising works. Not true. Clearly positioned and consistent advertising does work, though it is mainly supportive rather than the clinching argument for customers. Consider McDonald's. They make a deliberate attempt to meet 105 percent of their customers' expectations, not more, not less. People do not like surprises. You know that McDonald's will have clean rest rooms and fast service at a low price. You know just what to expect, and they deliver. They advertise what they actually provide, not more, not less.

The third myth is that, "you can save money by doing your own advertising." This is a costly mistake made by many beginners. Ineffective advertising is expensive. Advertising that does work, that informs your markets honestly, accurately and effectively, is worth its apparently high initial costs. Advertising includes signage, logos, stationery and business cards, everything that the public gets as an image of your restaurant. Your image and positioning are far too important to do yourself. And besides, you have a restaurant to run.

Hire a professional advertising agency or consultant to set up your advertising campaigns. It pays off. Check with your local SCORE or ACE chapter; they may have a professional who will help you in these matters for free. Check with the nearest college (including junior college) business program; they may have free or low-cost help for you. But do not try to do it yourself.

Some more questions to answer:

    1. What is the size of your markets?
    2. What percent of the market do you (will you) have?
    3. What is the market's growth potential?
    4. As the market grows, will your share (percentage) increase or decrease?
    5. Is the market competitive? If not, why not?

You can obtain information on the size of your markets from chambers of commerce, trade publications, marketing consultants, other business people, schools and colleges. The *Federal Census Report*, which will be in your local library, provides detailed information down to a block-by-block analysis of buying patterns for most areas.

Get help in assessing your prospective markets from such sources rather than trying to guess by watching passing traffic and hoping for the best. Good marketing strategies are planned. Good plans are based on good information.

VI. Pricing

Pricing is a widely misunderstood strategic tool. Lack of courage in pricing may be the biggest single marketing error small-business owners make. There is a widely held perception that price drives all purchasing decisions, so in order to gain market share you have to slash prices below the competition. Wrong! This is the worst strategy possible. You cannot afford to be the low-cost producer or cut-rate king.

Price and perceived value work together. Price is important. But it is not the only reason people buy things.

Look at it this way. Do you buy everything on price? Medical care? Cars? Food? Education for your children? You will find the following kind of matrix helpful in thinking through your pricing strategies.

Locate your restaurant and your competitors' restaurants on this matrix. You might also want to consider other factors besides quality, for instance convenience, ambiance, service or exclusivity (snob appeal). All of these influence price and perceived value.

Pricing Note

Pricing is a major marketing concern. Price, quality, service and profitability are tied together in a complex web. While there are some mechanical formulas for cranking out price decisions, there are a few common sense guidelines that will help you develop a price range to work within.

a. Price = Product + Service + Image + Expenses + Profit. The menu prices you set should reflect not only the cost of food itself but also an intangible image factor. In an ideal situation, you would know how your customers and prospects perceive the value of what you sell and price accordingly. You also have to cover costs and profits.

b. Determine your pricing objectives. Identify your objectives. Are you trying to buy market share with low prices? (It won't work but you can always try!) Maximize profits? Remain competitive? Build up a new product line? Your general marketing objectives apply here. Pricing is inherently strategic, so be clear on your objectives.

c. Establish price ranges. This is defensive. Make sure that you charge enough to cover your costs. A break-even analysis (see Section Two: Financial Data) will help you establish the low end of your price range. You have to cover your fixed costs with enough margin to survive, and this can be calculated in terms of both unit sales and dollars, thus helping you establish minimum prices.

At the high end, build your desired profit levels into the break-even equation and compare the prices you arrive at (on an item-by-item basis) to your sense of what the market will bear. Your customers won't pay more for your goods and services than they have to, and their perception of the value of your goods and services makes a very effective upper price limit.

d. Choose a flexible pricing approach. The four basic pricing approaches are full-cost pricing (which reflects your costs), flexible markups, gross margin pricing (which takes operating costs and marketing factors into account) and suggested or going rate. The last of these is the least desirable; it involves an endless game of follow-the-leader and ignores your cost structures. All of these approaches have their merits, however, and it makes sense for you to follow them.

The traditional method of pricing menu items is based upon "food cost" (or food cost percentage), which refers to the cost of the raw food ingredients expressed as a percentage of the selling price and is computed by the following formula:

Food Cost (Food Cost Percentage) =
(Cost of Raw Food Ingredients ÷ Selling Price) x 100

Example
Stefanie's Restaurant computes the cost of all the ingredients to make a single portion of Chicken Parker to be $2.35. In addition, the "Q" for a meal is $1.47, so the total cost for an order of Chicken Parker of $3.82. ("Q" refers to the "Quotient" or the cost of all other food items served with an entree. Stefanie's Restaurant includes a starch, a vegetable, a tossed salad, and bread and butter with each entree at no additional cost. Thus, the cost of food includes not only the cost of the entree, but the "Q" factor or the cost of all the other food items included with the price of the entree.) Since Chicken Parker sells for $9.95, the "Food Cost" of Chicken Parker is:

Food Cost (Food Cost Percentage)
= (Cost of Raw Food Ingredients ÷ Selling Price) x 100
= ($3.82 ÷ $9.95) x 100
= .384 x 100
= 38.4 %

Restaurants traditionally determine their desired food cost percentage and compute a selling price based upon the cost of raw food ingredients and the desired food cost percentage. Dividing the cost of raw food ingredients by the desired food cost percentage provides the suggested selling price. In the case of Chicken Parker, the suggested selling price of the menu item, based on a desired 40 percent food cost, is $9.55 which was computed as follows:

Suggested Selling Price =
Cost of Raw Food Ingredients ÷ Desired Food Cost Percentage =
$3.82 ÷ 0.40 = $9.55

Thus, Stefanie's Restaurant should sell Chicken Parker for $9.55 per portion if it wants to obtain a 40 percent food cost. In fact, Stefanie's Restaurant sells the item for $9.95, which results in a food cost of 38.4 percent. The reason for increasing the price was to compensate for the amount of labor required to prepare the item and the fact that the owner felt the market would perceive a greater value in the product and would pay a slightly higher price.

Table 1 shows the computations used by Stefanie's Restaurant to determine the suggested selling price of each menu item, the actual selling price, and the food cost percentage based upon the actual selling price.

Table 2 shows how Stefanie's Restaurant then determined the gross profit for each item by subtracting the cost of raw food for each item from the selling price for each item.

Finally, Table 3 shows the computation for the overall targeted food cost. Since each item has a slightly different food cost percentage, and since all items are not uniformly popular, the overall food cost percentage must be computed by weighing the individual percentages by the number of items sold. Table 3 shows the number of items sold and computes overall food cost percentage based upon popularity of items.

For a fuller description of these pricing approaches, check with your accountant. A review of your pricing strategy is a valuable addition to planning, and should be part of your periodic financial and accounting reviews.

VII. Goals and Budgets

In Section Two: Financial Data, you will establish budgets that include money for marketing. The amount you budget for advertising (the most visible but by no means most important part of marketing) depends on what you are trying to accomplish for your restaurant.

A start-up restaurant needs to spend more for marketing than a well-established restaurant since the markets need to be informed that you are in business, where and when, and what products or services you will provide. A very rough guide to marketing expenditures can be gained by looking at trade figures, but keep in mind that the average percentage of gross sales (a common measure) is based on a wide range of restaurants with different markets, different positioning with-

Table 1:
Stefanie's Restaurant
Computation of Selling Price
and Food Cost Percentage by Menu Item

	"Q"	Other Food	Total Raw Food Cost $	Suggested Selling Price at 40% Food Cost	Actual Selling Price	Food Cost %
Entrees						
Fran's Shrimp	1.47	2.66	4.13	10.33	10.95	37.7%
Charbroiled Chicken	1.47	1.50	2.97	7.43	9.95	29.8%
Seafood Platter	1.47	3.58	5.05	12.63	12.95	39.0%
Baked Haddock	1.47	2.00	3.47	8.68	8.95	38.8%
N. Y. Strip	1.47	3.22	4.69	11.73	12.95	36.2%
Striptease	1.47	2.38	3.85	9.63	7.95	48.4%
Mate's Delmonico	1.47	2.30	3.77	9.43	10.95	34.4%
Captain's Delmonico	1.47	3.22	4.69	11.73	12.95	36.2%
Veggie Lasagna	1.47	1.82	3.29	8.23	8.95	36.8%
Chicken Parker	1.47	2.35	3.82	9.55	9.95	38.4%
BBQ Spare Ribs	1.47	1.60	3.07	7.68	9.95	30.9%
Voo Doo Chicken	1.47	1.60	3.07	7.68	9.95	30.9%
Voo Doo & Ribs	1.47	1.90	3.37	8.43	10.95	30.8%
Queen Prime Rib	1.47	2.68	4.15	10.38	10.95	37.9%
King Prime Rib	1.47	3.12	4.59	11.48	12.95	35.4%
Fried Haddock	1.47	2.60	4.07	10.18	9.95	40.9%
Crab Legs	1.47	2.25	3.72	9.30	9.95	37.4%
Sandwiches						
Boater's Burger		1.19	1.19	2.98	3.95	30.1%
Fisherman		1.30	1.30	3.25	3.50	37.1%
Char. Chicken		1.12	1.12	2.80	3.50	32.0%
Voo Doo Chicken		1.14	1.14	2.85	3.50	32.6%
Chicken Tenders		1.45	1.45	3.63	3.25	44.6%
Chicken in Basket		1.85	1.85	4.63	4.75	38.9%
Hot Dog		0.87	0.87	2.18	2.75	31.6%

"Q"
Baked Potato*	0.10
French Fries*	0.40
Onion Rings*	0.48
Vegetable	0.10
Tossed Salad	0.44
Bread & Butter	0.45
Highest Total	1.47

* Only one of these three is served with an entree.

Section One: The Business

Table 2:
Stefanie's Restaurant
Computation of Gross Profit and
Computation of Food Cost Percentage by Menu Item

	"Q"	Other Food	Total Food $	Selling Price	Gross Profit	Food Cost %
Entrees						
Fran's Shrimp	1.47	2.66	4.13	10.95	6.82	37.7%
Charbroiled Chicken	1.47	1.50	2.97	9.95	6.98	29.8%
Seafood Platter	1.47	3.58	5.05	12.95	7.90	39.0%
Baked Haddock	1.47	2.00	3.47	8.95	5.48	38.8%
N. Y. Strip	1.47	3.22	4.69	12.95	8.26	36.2%
Striptease	1.47	2.38	3.85	7.95	4.10	48.4%
Mate's Delmonico	1.47	2.30	3.77	10.95	7.18	34.4%
Captain's Delmonico	1.47	3.22	4.69	12.95	8.26	36.2%
Veggie Lasagna	1.47	1.82	3.29	8.95	5.66	36.8%
Chicken Parker	1.47	2.35	3.82	9.95	6.13	38.4%
BBQ Spare Ribs	1.47	1.60	3.07	9.95	6.88	30.9%
Voo Doo Chicken	1.47	1.60	3.07	9.95	6.88	30.9%
Voo Doo & Ribs	1.47	1.90	3.37	10.95	7.58	30.8%
Queen Prime Rib	1.47	2.68	4.15	10.95	6.80	37.9%
King Prime Rib	1.47	3.12	4.59	12.95	8.36	35.4%
Fried Haddock	1.47	2.60	4.07	9.95	5.88	40.9%
Crab Legs	1.47	2.25	3.72	9.95	6.23	37.4%
Sandwiches						
Boater's Burger		1.19	1.19	3.95	2.76	30.1%
Fisherman		1.30	1.30	3.50	2.20	37.1%
Char. Chicken		1.12	1.12	3.50	2.38	32.0%
Voo Doo Chicken		1.14	1.14	3.50	2.36	32.6%
Chicken Tenders		1.45	1.45	3.25	1.80	44.6%
Chicken in Basket		1.85	1.85	4.75	2.90	38.9%
Hot Dog		0.87	0.87	2.75	1.88	31.6%

"Q"
Baked Potato*	0.10
French Fries*	0.40
Onion Rings*	0.48
Vegetable	0.10
Tossed Salad	0.44
Bread & Butter	0.45
Highest Total	1.47

* Only one of these three is served with an entree.

Table 3: Stefanie's Restaurant Computation of Overall Food Cost

	Food Cost $ Single Portion	Number Portions Sold	Total Food Cost $	Selling Price	Number Portions Sold	Total Income $
Entrees						
Fran's Shrimp	4.13	2	8.26	10.95	2	21.90
Charbroiled Chicken	2.97	7	20.79	9.95	7	69.65
Seafood Platter	5.05	3	15.15	12.95	3	38.85
Baked Haddock	3.47	2	6.94	8.95	2	17.90
N. Y. Strip	4.69	2	9.38	12.95	2	25.90
Striptease	3.85	4	15.40	7.95	4	31.80
Mate's Delmonico	3.77	5	18.85	10.95	5	54.75
Captain's Delmonico	4.69	4	18.76	12.95	4	51.80
Veggie Lasagna	3.29	2	6.58	8.95	2	17.90
Chicken Parker	3.82	3	11.46	9.95	3	29.85
BBQ Spare Ribs	3.07	2	6.14	9.95	2	19.90
Voo Doo Chicken	3.07	6	18.42	9.95	6	59.70
Voo Doo & Ribs	3.37	2	6.74	10.95	2	21.90
Queen Prime Rib	4.15	4	16.60	10.95	4	43.80
King Prime Rib	4.59	3	13.77	12.95	3	38.85
Fried Haddock	4.07	5	20.35	9.95	5	49.75
Crab Legs	3.72	4	14.88	9.95	4	39.80
Sandwiches						
Boater's Burger	1.19	10	11.90	3.95	10	39.50
Fisherman	1.30	9	11.70	3.50	9	31.50
Char. Chicken	1.12	5	5.60	3.50	5	17.50
Voo Doo Chicken	1.14	6	6.84	3.50	6	21.00
Chicken Tenders	1.45	4	5.80	3.25	4	13.00
Chicken in Basket	1.85	4	7.40	4.75	4	19.00
Hot Dog	0.87	2	1.74	2.75	2	5.50
Totals		**100**	**279.45**		**100**	**781.00**

Overall Food Cost % = (cost of Raw Food Ingredients ÷ Selling Price) x 100
= ($279.45 ÷ 781.00) x 100
= 35.8%

in those markets, and at different stages in their life cycles. A restaurant milking a cash cow will spend less than a restaurant aggressively seeking a share of a new market.

Your safest course is to look at your sales and profit goals, then work backward to see what marketing goals and budgets will help you reach those sales and profit levels. Your goals might include training waiters and bartenders, opening a new restaurant in another city, or changing your menus dramatically. The key point: tie your marketing goals and budgets to your restaurant's goals, not to an artificially chosen or arbitrary percentage of gross sales plucked from a trade or financial publication.

An old saw tells us, it takes money to make money. Your advertising and promotion budget is an investment in future sales, not an expense that can be cut at the slightest sign of a drop in profitability. Note that if you know your target market, and how to reach it, you can control some of these promotional costs, but in a brand-new market you would still have to get your message out more vigorously than to a market that knows your restaurant well. Think of all the steps there are in the Promotion Pyramid that you have to move brand-new customers along.

VIII. Strategies

Pick the simplest strategy you can. "Coddle your customer" is the best strategy for any small or new business. If put into effect it will automatically distinguish your restaurant from your competition, because most restaurants are run for the sake of the owner and employees, not the customer.

"Minimize opportunities for customer dissatisfaction" is another excellent strategy. It puts your customers where they belong, at the center of all your business efforts, and reminds you and your employees that the customer is the reason you are in business in the first place.

Why pick a simple strategy? Because simple strategies work. Complex strategies get shelved or miscommunicated. Napoléon always closeted himself with the dumbest general under his command, and explained to a jealous Maréchal Ney (his most brilliant general) that, "If he understands it, the dumbest private will...."

That's all you want from a strategy. Clear and complete communication with employees and markets, based on a comprehensive customer focus.

Finally, your strategy has to address these two questions:
  1. **How will you attract and keep your target markets?**
  2. **How can you profitably expand your market niche(s)?**

Most restaurants are run for the sake of the owner and employees, not the customer.

These bring in such further questions as how and where to advertise, the suitability of your location, the attractiveness and accessibility of your location, and the fit between your restaurant and its chosen markets. You can't answer them without knowing your markets in great detail, which presupposes that you have gone to the trouble of first defining, then segmenting your markets.

Use your mission statement to test your strategy. This is easy to do: State your strategy, then see if it advances your mission. If the answer is no, discard it.

Think of McDonald's. Their motto (a statement of their mission) is QSC&V: Quality, Service, Cleanliness and Value. Constant and consistent reference to QSC&V guarantees that all of their activities have a customer-centered marketing focus.

A Sample Description of the Market
Stefanie's Restaurant will continue to provide freshly prepared food in a casual, attractive setting to both local residents and tourists. We plan to increase our seasonal business by expanding our capacity and identifying our customers to develop direct marketing campaigns to attract repeat business during the off season.

Our goal is to provide quality food and service at competitive prices to customers within 20 miles of Anytown. This market has a total population of over 50,000 people.

Customers will be attracted by:
- direct mail to previous patrons;
- a local radio and newspaper advertising campaign;
- word-of-mouth advertising from our present customer base; and
- our location and signs on Route X, a heavily traveled tourist route.

Note that Stefanie's Restaurant has included strategies consistent with the policy stated in the above example. Stefanie's marketing strategy is limited to a specific geographical area, from which they feel they can entice people to travel. Their advertising will be on local radio stations (four 1000-kw FM stations cover the area) and in local papers. Advertising can be costly, and they plan to invest their advertising budget wisely.

Stefanie's pricing strategy is pegged to competitive prices. This strategy is questionable since they pay top dollar for their product and provide a superior level of service. They could justify a higher price, on the basis of higher quality, better service and their lakeside location.

D. Location of Business

Proper site location is critical to the success of your restaurant. A number of studies have indicated that the three major reasons for small business failure are lack of management expertise, undercapitalization, and location. Ellsworth M. Statler, the innovative hotelier, when asked what the three most important factors in the success of his hotels were, is credited with responding, "location, location, location." Over the years, the same response has been attributed to restaurants and retail stores, among others. First try to locate the ideal site, then figure out how close you can come to it.

Information about specific areas is available from chambers of commerce, industrial development commissions (they may also have information about tax breaks and financing incentives for businesses that will employ substantial numbers of people in towns under their commission), trade sources such as magazines and associations, planning commissions, bankers, and lawyers. Try these first. Then ask commercial real estate brokers, once you have a feel for how much space you need, and about location cost requirements.

Do not open a restaurant in a given spot simply because the price is low. Rent and purchase prices are fixed by market forces, and a low price usually reflects low desirability. Remember—the three most important success factors are said to be location, location and location!

Different types of restaurants have different needs. What is your target market? If you want to attract a large breakfast business, then you should be located on the side of the road that commuters travel on their way to work in the morning. On the other hand, if your target is dinner business, your restaurant should be located on the side of the road the commuters travel on their way home in the evening. If you are looking to specialize in the lunch business, then a downtown location within walking distance of office buildings may be the ideal.

There are also a number of other questions you should consider when looking for the ideal location. What are the traffic counts and at what hours? Is the location visible from the road? Is there adequate parking? Are there restrictive zoning ordinances either for the type of business or the hours of operation? Is there easy access (second floor locations are not well received by restaurant patrons)? Can renovations be made inexpensively or at all? (E.g., some codes require venting of kitchen equipment straight through the ceiling rather than through a wall. The cost may become excessive—or the task impossible—if you attempt to install venting in the first floor of a six-story office building.)

Your banker may be your most helpful reference. Some locations seem to be jinxed, and bankers are apt to know why and will tell you.

Do not open a restaurant in a given spot simply because the price is low.

In this section of your business plan, you should answer the following questions:

1. **What is your restaurant's address?**
2. **What are the physical features of your building?**
3. **Do you lease or own your space?**
4. **What renovations are needed, and how much will they cost?** Get written quotes from more than one contractor. Include these as supporting documents.
5. **What equipment will be needed and how much will it cost?** Get written bids from more than one supplier and don't forget to include installation and freight-in costs. Include these as supporting documents.
6. **Does zoning permit your kind of business in the neighborhood?**
7. **What other businesses (kinds of businesses) are in the area?** For example, car dealers tend to cluster. So do restaurants (especially fast-food restaurants), jewelry stores, art businesses and financial businesses.
8. **Why did you pick this site over others?**
9. **Why is this the right location for your restaurant?**
10. **How will the choice of location affect your operating costs?** A bad site can put you out of business, while a good site will increase your profits. Choose wisely.

Once you get started, or if you are already in a good location, keep a constant eye on changes in your location—new roads get built, populations change, people move, zoning ordinances change, and your business needs may change too. Prepare to anticipate these changes. Compare census reports over a period of time to find long-term shifts. Keep in touch with real estate people who have to know what's happening.

A Sample Description of the Location

Stefanie's Restaurant is currently leasing a two-story, log cabin building (3,000 square feet) with commercial kitchen at 123 Main Street, Anytown, NY, for $1,200 per month with an option to renew the lease annually at the same rent for the next five years. The site is zoned for commercial use and has frontage and docking facilities (for up to 20 boats) on Lake Delaney. Main Street is a heavily traveled summer tourist route and Stefanie's Restaurant is one of only two restaurants accessible by boat. Stefanie's Restaurant has performed major leasehold improvements, and is planning to install an outdoor dining deck, which will be partially covered with a tent and two additional rest rooms. All necessary commercial equipment to function as a restaurant is in place. The building is divided into two dining rooms, a bar with fireplace lounge for dining, a commercial kitchen with appropriate storage equipment and facilities, and an office. See the diagram on page 116.

This section needn't be too involved. Except for serving as a reminder of things to look out for, once the location has been chosen a brief statement is all that's necessary when you update your business plan. Suggested alterations may not be made between periods of updating your plan, so it may be wise to make a note of them as they come up.

Section One: The Business

E. The Competition

If you have decided on your target markets and found that they are large enough to be profitable and contain reasonable expansion possibilities, the next step is to check out your competition, both direct (those operations similar to yours) and indirect.

There are three times you should be concerned about the competition.

1. When you are planning to start up or buy a restaurant, or planning to enter a market that's new (to you). You'd better check up on the competition before sitting down with your investors and banker—because the first question they'll probably ask is, "What competition do you face?" The restaurant business is inherently competitive, and since there is very little that's new in business, most worthwhile markets are already being worked by someone. In fact, if you think you've found a brand new untapped market, think carefully before entering it. If there are no competitors, it's probably because the market can't support a restaurant.

2. When a new competitor arrives on the scene. When you study the competition under these circumstances, you probably won't have the flexibility you had earlier. New competition can come from direct competitors (old rivals as well as new ones). But it can also come from outside the traditional restaurant industry. Supermarkets are now selling ready-to-eat meals.

3. All the time. This ongoing monitoring of the competition is an inexpensive form of preventive maintenance, and is your best strategy for protecting your customer base. While forestalling competition and ensuring your survival is very important, being in a position to recognize and take advantage of new opportunities is even more important. Constant monitoring of the market will allow you to keep ahead of your competition, whether new or old.

To analyze your competition, consider the following questions:

1. Who are your five nearest competitors?
2. How is their business—steady, increasing or decreasing?
3. How are their operations similar and dissimilar to yours?
4. What have you learned from watching their operation? What works for them? What doesn't?
5. How will your restaurant be better than theirs?

To make gathering this information easy, set up competitor files, simple manila folders into which you put any scrap of information about your competitors. You will be surprised how quickly you gain a clear picture of what your competition is up to. Collect and date their ads, brochures, trade show handouts and any other printed material. Jot down their radio jingles. Put in notes of rumors about their financial

If there are no competitors, it's probably because the market can't support a restaurant.

condition, want ads, activities in the community. Anything that helps you form a clear picture of their plans is germane.

Then review each competitor file weekly or monthly. This has to be done systematically or the full benefits will be lost. Who are they advertising to? How? What are they trying to sell? The benefits they stress will be a good indicator. Where do they advertise? And so on.

The objective of this section is to enable you to pick up the good competitive practices of your competitors and avoid their errors. Carefully viewing the competition can lead you to alter your basic strategy or to change existing operations to compete more effectively. This has to be an ongoing practice since dining trends are continually changing and success attracts competitors.

How should you compete? Knowledgeably. There are many alternatives to price competition, for example, that restaurateurs could profitably use. These are based on knowing how your restaurant compares to competing restaurants.

You won't be able to fight on every front. Choose the areas where you can gain a competitive advantage, one based on your restaurant's strengths (people, product and service are the three most important). Try to match your strengths against your competitors' weaknesses—which of course means you have to know what these matchups are. For a quick comparison, fill in the following form.

Customer Seeks:	Competition Offers:	You offer:
Quality		
Exclusivity		
Lower prices		
Menu selections		
Service (quality)		
Service (speed)		
Delivery		
Location		
Parking		
Atmosphere		
Credit cards		
Space for private parties		
Service (type)		
Service (attitude)		

The number of competitors (five) mentioned in question one is arbitrary. Use your own judgment. But make sure to regularly keep abreast of the competition. Business—any business—is too competitive to allow your attention to lapse.

A Sample Description of the Competition

There are three restaurant operations competing directly with Stefanie's Restaurant.

1. Nikki's Place—is the only other restaurant located on Lake Delaney with docking facilities. Nikki's Place is located in Major City, 16 miles to the south of Stefanie's Restaurant, which is the major population center of the area and the location of most of the marinas. Nikki's Place has a larger population to draw from during the off season, but during the summer, Stefanie's Restaurant is more desirable since it offers a better experience—an hour boat ride from the marinas (rather than a one-minute boat ride) or a 20-minute drive along the shore of the lake. During the winter, Nikki's Place has a more advantageous location.

2. Mr. D's Bowling Alley—is located in Anytown, three miles from the lakefront. Mr. D's is open for dinner and snacks six nights a week all year and caters mainly to local residents. Their average check is considerably lower than Stefanie's and the atmosphere is more casual and louder. Mr. D's does an excellent business but competes for a different market than does Stefanie's Restaurant.

3. Happy Times—is a diner located two miles from Stefanie's, away from the water. Happy Times is open for three meals a day, seven days a week. It has just opened under new ownership after being closed for almost six years.

Indirect competition during the summer season comes from almost 40 restaurants in Major City, 16 miles south of Stefanie's Restaurant. However, these restaurants have a much more competitive location during the winter season.

Ninety-eight percent of small-business failures are avoidable.

F. Management

According to various studies of factors involved in small-business failures, 98 percent of the failures stem from three major causes: lack of management expertise, undercapitalization, and location. Two percent of the failures are due to factors beyond control of the people involved. Restaurants are no exception.

Your business plan must take this into account. If you are preparing a financing proposal, you should make sure that your prospective financing source is aware of what steps you have taken or are taking to correct any weakness in your managerial staff (yourself and any other managerial people involved); if you are to use your business plan to its fullest, you should use this segment to highlight both strengths and weaknesses of management for your own sake.

The failure factor breakdown for lack of managerial expertise provides a guide:

Managerial incompetence	45%
Inexperience in the line	9%
Inexperience in management	18%
Unbalanced expertise	20%
Neglect of business	3%
Fraud	2%
Disaster	1%
Total:	98%

There is no known cure for incompetence, but there are two very direct cures for inexperience and/or unbalanced experience: Get the necessary experience yourself; get a partner or employee who has the requisite experience. (An important Small Business Administration study showed a high correlation between small business success and having a partner as opposed to being a solo act.)

The final three items represent managerial failures because neglect of business, fraud, or being put out of business by disaster could almost always have been prevented by foresight. Insurance, for example, can protect a business against both fraud and disaster, while neglect of business is a form of business suicide.

In preparing the management section, there are five areas to cover:

1. **Personal History of the Principals**
2. **Related Work Experience**
3. **Duties and Responsibilities**
4. **Salaries**
5. **Resources Available to the Business**

Section One: The Business

Personal History of Principals
This segment should include responses to the following questions:

1. What is your business background?
2. What restaurant management experience have you had?
3. What education (including both formal and informal learning experiences) has a bearing on your managerial abilities?
4. What is (are) your age(s), special abilities and interests, reasons for going into business, where do you live and have you lived, and so on. The personal data needn't be a confession, but it should reflect where your motivation comes from. Without a lot of motivation, your chances of success are slight. It pays to be ruthlessly honest with yourself—even if you don't put the results on paper.
5. **Are you physically up to the job?** Stamina counts. The restaurant business requires long hours and is physically demanding.
6. **Why are you going to be successful in this restaurant?** Keep in mind that your family will be affected by your decision to go into the restaurant business. Try to assess the potential fallout—while your family may be supportive now, will they continue to be when you're putting in 80-hour weeks, including nights and weekends, for very little money?
7. **What is your personal financial status?** A personal balance sheet must be included as a supporting document in your business plan if the plan is to double as a financing proposal.

Bankers and other providers of capital want to see as much collateral as possible to secure their investment. There are no restaurant loans; there are only loans to restaurant owners, and under most circumstances the personal credit worthiness of the principals will be the major factor in your banker's decision. Many banks won't even consider loaning money for restaurants.

You will undoubtedly be expected to personally guarantee the loan. This means that your personal assets may be taken if the restaurant fails—even if the business is a corporation. Your banker doesn't want to be in the secondhand house business, but centuries of experience indicate that if you are personally tied to the business, you'll be less apt to walk away from it if things get tight.

There are no restaurant loans; there are only loans to restaurant owners.

Related Work Experience
This segment is a detailed response to the experience factors mentioned earlier. It includes (but is not limited to) responses to the following:

1. What is your direct operational experience in the restaurant business?
2. What is your managerial experience in business in general and the restaurant business in particular?
3. What other managerial experience have you had—in different businesses, in a club or on a team, in civic or religious organizations, or in some other area? Many managerial skills are transferable. Others

are not, but the more evidence and analysis of your managerial experience you can show, the better. You'll be able to use this to plug managerial gaps.

Unbalanced managerial experience can cause serious problems. For example, the talents required of a financial specialist are quite different from those required to run your restaurant. The combination of both sets of talent in one individual is rare.

Duties and Responsibilities

Once you have written down the experience and skills (and have a feel for the weaknesses) of the proposed management, this segment becomes much simpler. Follow the rule: Always build on strengths and seek to alleviate weaknesses.

This is a variant of, "you can't make a silk purse out of a sow's ear"—attempting to make a salesman out of a retiring clerk is folly. Attempting to make a chef out of a salesman is also folly. Use skills to advantage.

The most scarce asset you will have is time. To make the most of it, make sure that you budget your time carefully by spelling out, in advance:

- who does what;
- who reports to whom; and
- who makes the final decisions.

Make sure you allot adequate time for:

1. Planning and reviewing plans;
2. Major operating duties (purchasing, sales, personnel, production, promotion and advertising, marketing, and so forth as needed in your restaurant); and
3. More planning.

The purpose of your business plan is to make your restaurant run more smoothly, more profitably and more easily. If you find that you spend a lot of time solving yesterday's problems, stop. Get out of the restaurant, sit down somewhere quiet and begin to plan. That time investment—anywhere from a few hours to a few days—can make all the difference.

Allocating duties and responsibilities is critical. If the chain of command is unclear to your employees, you will have the worst kinds of personnel problems. This is a major management responsibility and must not be evaded under the hopeful guise of "we can work it out later when we see where the problems are." By then it will be too late.

Section One: The Business

Salaries

A simple statement of what the management will be paid is sufficient. Just remember to cut the fat from your personal budget, add 15 percent for contingencies, and then stick to it. Many deals never get going because bankers feel the principals are getting paid more than they should; other deals self-destruct when the rock-bottom salary figures, unrealistic to begin with, are altered without planning, thus throwing the budgets into disarray. Be realistic. Don't be greedy. Your payoff comes in the future, after your restaurant becomes successful.

To help you figure out what you need to live on, we have provided some cost of living budget forms in Appendix Five.

Knowing what you need, as distinguished from thinking you know what you need, takes effort, but one sure way to damage a small business is to bleed it for family necessities. If your restaurant can't afford to pay you a living wage, and you have no other income or savings, you better think your deal over again.

If you are preparing a financing plan, your banker will need the cost of living budget to help justify your salary requirements. Remember: be realistic.

Resources Available to the Business

All businesses, no matter how tiny, need:
1. an accountant;
2. a lawyer;
3. a banker; and
4. an insurance agent or broker.

If you have to be told why you need these, you shouldn't be contemplating going into business.

Other sources of assistance include:
5. Chambers of commerce, regional planning commissions and councils.
6. Business, trade, and civic organizations.
7. Small Business Administration technical assistance, ACE and SCORE, SBDC and SBI programs.
8. Consultants.
9. Colleges, universities and schools.
10. Federal, state and local agencies.
11. Your board of directors.
12. The local, state, and national restaurant associations.

Don't forget: Your banker can be among the most helpful of all due to the nature of the job. Bankers trade in information as much as in credit, and banks have a wealth of information about businesses, which you can tap simply by asking.

Banks have a wealth of information about businesses' which you can tap simply by asking.

You won't have to use all of these resources (except the first four), but it is a good idea to know what help will be available if you need it, and to know where it is (and who it is) well ahead of time.

List these resources, and make yourself known to them. You can plug many gaps in your experience and increase your chances of success by relying on other people's experience. Tapping into many of these resources will cost you no more than time and a phone call.

• • •

This section is intended to make you aware of the availability of management skills in and outside your restaurant. If you keep in mind the necessity of managing your restaurant rather than letting your restaurant manage you (and constantly review and reevaluate the results of this analysis in the future), you will drastically reduce the odds against you. Keep this section short, direct, and honest.

A Sample Description of Management

Stefanie Clark was born in Anytown, NY, and has lived there most of her life. After graduating from local schools, she attended Verbeyst University where she graduated with a four-year degree in hotel management. During high school and college, she worked part-time and during the summers at a variety of local restaurants as a busgirl, waitress, hostess, and dining room supervisor. She also took several food production courses during her college career.

After graduating from college, Stefanie worked as the assistant manager of a high-volume restaurant at a ski resort and summer camp in Wyoming for three years. She then worked for four years as assistant manager and unit manager for Surf 'N Turf, a national restaurant chain. Ms. Clark started Stefanie's Restaurant one year ago when she leased the building and invested $20,000 of her own savings and $10,000 that she borrowed from her parents. She is unmarried and shares an apartment in Anytown with two other women.

To augment her management skills, Ms. Clark hired Tage Farrell, a recent graduate of the American Culinary School, to operate and to manage the kitchen. Although Tage is young, he desires to have his own restaurant someday and is grateful for the opportunity to work closely with someone of Stefanie's talent and experience. Both are healthy and energetic and want to see the restaurant succeed.

Stefanie's salary was $1,000 a month for the first year in order to enable the business to pay off start-up costs as quickly as possible. She intends to take a salary of $1,200 during the second year with any profits returned to the business to reduce debt and finance expansion.

In order to augment her skills, Stefanie has enlisted the help of Furey & Fey (CPAs), Chris Sterling (lawyer), and Bill Witt, a retired banker who will be on her advisory board. Other advisory board members are Andrew O'Bangfo, business consultant, Verbeyst University's Venture Incubator Division's Louis Dora, and Fran Teetom of FROG (Female Restaurateurs Organized for Growth). This board will provide ongoing management review.

G. Personnel

Personnel management is a major stumbling block for restaurant owners. Personnel management is a demanding profession that few people learn; the assumption that "I can manage people because I've been around" is dangerous. You may find it valuable to hire a consultant to set up your personnel systems, help in hiring and training, and educate you in personnel management. While the cost may seem high initially, the cost of a poor hiring process can be catastrophic. Remember: Your employees will be representing your restaurant to your patrons!

Businesses stand or fall on the strength of their personnel. Good employees can make a marginal business succeed; poor or dishonest employees can destroy the best restaurant.

Restaurants stand or fall on the strength of their personnel.

As with other management tasks, personnel management requires careful planning. Here are some questions to think about as you outline your personnel needs for the future:

1. What are your personnel needs now? In the near future? In five years?
2. What skills will your restaurant need?
3. Are the people with those skills available? Where?
4. Will you have full- or part-time employees?
5. Will your employees be salaried or hourly?
6. What fringe benefits will you offer?
7. Will you pay overtime?
8. Will you have to train people? If so, at what cost to your restaurant (time, interrupted work flow, money)? Be careful. Training can be a hidden cost that you didn't expect.

Hire people only when it will result in added profitability for your restaurant, and determine before hiring whether the job is really necessary. If it is, then careful selection of the right person for that job will pay off. Salaries are a fixed expense, and you want to be sure that the expense is really necessary.

A Sample Description of Personnel

Stefanie's Restaurant employs two full-time salaried employees on a year-round basis: a kitchen manager/chef at $400 per week, and a dining room manager/hostess at $350 per week. The restaurant also uses part-time permanent and seasonal employees as needed to meet its additional staffing requirements. There are enough people in the area who are willing to work part-time to meet the staffing needs during the winter months, and high school and college students are readily available during the peak summer season. The use of part-time and seasonal employees allows Stefanie's Restaurant to hire personnel according to their needs and helps to keep the labor costs in line with industry standards.

Stefanie's Restaurant
Staffing Schedule

Scheduled to Work

Position	9	10	11	12	1	2	3	4	5	6	7	8	9	10	11	Total Hours	Hourly Rate	Daily Pay
1st Cook					←——————————→											8	8.00	64.00
2nd Cook								←——————————→								8	6.50	52.00
Prep		←————→														6	5.50	33.00
Prep		←—————→														8	5.50	44.00
Prep								←——→								5	5.50	27.50
Dishwasher		←——→														6	4.50	27.00
Dishwasher							←————→									8	4.50	36.00
Dishwasher									←——→							6	4.50	27.00
Bartender			←—————→													8	4.50	36.00
Bartender									←——→							6	4.50	27.00
Hostess		←—————→														8	5.00	40.00
Hostess									←——→							6	5.00	30.00
Hostess																	5.00	0.00
Waitperson			←———→													8	4.25	34.00
Waitperson		←————→														8	4.25	34.00
Waitperson		←——→														5	4.25	29.75
Waitperson									←———→							7	4.25	29.75
Waitperson									←———→							7	4.25	29.75
Waitperson									←———→							7	4.25	29.75
Waitperson									←———→							7	4.25	29.75
Waitperson									←———→							7	4.25	29.75
Total																**139**		**$690.00**

Note: In addition to the above hourly employees, the kitchen manager/cook and the dining room manager are salaried employees at $400 and $350 per week respectively.

An example of a staffing schedule is included on page 46. The sample shown is for a single day at peak demand. Similar schedules are prepared for days with less than peak demand. When taken together, the staffing schedules provide excellent control of overall labor costs.

H. Application and Expected Effect of Loan

This section is important whether you are seeking a loan, outside equity or planning to finance your deal yourself. In determining how much money you'll need and for what purposes it will be used, do not rely on guesses when exact prices or firm estimates are available. If you must make an estimate, specify how you arrived at your figures.

It is often helpful to make a three-column list.

Bare Bones (What you can just scrape by with—secondhand, makeshift—the bare minimum.)	Reasonable (What you will most likely get—some new, some used, some fancy, some plain.)	Optimal (What you'd like if money were no problem.)
1. Ten cinder blocks and wire grill set up on lawn with charcoal to broil steaks. (Cost = $12.50)	Used 24" (48,000 BTU) natural gas charbroiler available from Maguire's Used Restaurant Equipment. (Cost = $261.00 + installation)	New 34" (72,000 BTU) natural gas charbroiler available from Barr's Hi Speed Kitchen Equipment. (Cost = $866.00 + installation)
2. Used desk ($7.00)	Inexpensive desk ($55)	New teak desk ($750)

Fill out the Bare Bones and Optimal columns first, then make your reasonable choice. It may be important for you to have a luxury item or two, but weigh the cost. This tabular worksheet is particularly handy for a start-up business and can be used whenever a purchase of additional equipment is contemplated.

Make sure that this section contains responses to the following:

  1. How is the loan or investment to be spent? This can be fairly general (working capital and new equipment, inventory, supplies, and so on).
  2. What items will be purchased?
  3. Who is the supplier?
  4. What is the price?
  5. What is the specific model name and/or number of your purchase?
  6. How much did you (will you) pay in sales tax, installation charges, freight or delivery fees? Your banker may be interested in using whatever it is you are buying as collateral for the loan. By having a list, your loan can be processed faster.
  You should consider the possible advantages of leasing some of the capital equipment you need and definitely look into the advantages of renting rather than owning your place of business. If you have the

money to buy, owning may (or may not—ask your accountant) be less expensive than leasing. If you are short of cash, a lease arrangement may enable you to ease your cash problems by lowering your investment in fixed assets (perhaps a sale/lease back deal would help if you already own the building).

Leases also have great flexibility: as your restaurant grows, you may want to change some of the fixed assets. Leases also have certain tax advantages. Once more, check with your accountant.

Most importantly, ask yourself:

7. How will the loan make your restaurant more profitable?

Interest is an expense that directly reduces profits. If you propose borrowing money or investing your own, you must know how well that money will work for you.

Make sure the loan earns more than it costs.

The exact figures in the Application and Expected Effect of the Loan or Investment section won't be available until you have worked through the financial data, but the fixed assets you plan to acquire and some working capital needs can and should be addressed here. You can always pare back from Reasonable to Bare Bones (for example) if your finances demand it.

If you propose borrowing money or investing your own, you must know how well that money will work for you.

A Sample of Application and Expected Effect of Loan or Investment

The $35,000 will be used as follows:

Leasehold improvements

Construct 1,764 sq. ft. dining deck	$12,000
Construct additional rest rooms (See contractor's estimate included in Appendix)	10,000
Tent (Farrell's Tent Co.)	3,500
Tables and Chairs for 100	2,000
Kitchen Equipment	1,000
Inventories (China, Silver, Glassware)	1,500
Cash Reserve	5,000
Total Needed	$35,000
Less: Additional Equity Investment	($10,000)
Proceeds from Loan	**$25,000**

Stefanie's Restaurant can increase its capacity at a time when there is excess demand by constructing a dining deck. Since the excess demand is during the summer months when the weather is good, the dining deck provides extra seating at a minimal cost compared to constructing a fully enclosed building. The deck should also provide Stefanie's Restaurant with an additional competitive advantage in the summer months since no other restaurant in the area offers outdoor dining. The deck will also keep insurance costs low and will not have to be heated during the winter months when it is not needed.

The additional rest rooms are needed for two reasons. First, the existing rest rooms are not large enough to handle the current level of business, let alone any increased patronage; and second, because of their location, people waiting to use the existing facilities interfere with the flow of traffic between the dining room and the kitchen.

The tent is needed to provide shade for those patrons who desire it and also to provide shelter for diners in the event that a sudden rainstorm develops when the restaurant is full. There would not be room to move 100 additional customers inside on a busy night.

The additional inventories and kitchen equipment are needed to accommodate the 100 additional people seated at any one time.

The bank will hold the reserve as a line of credit. It will be used to take advantage of special opportunities or to meet emergencies.

The example is modest. For a more complicated deal, much more detail would be needed. Be guided by your judgment in this section. The hard figures in the Financial Data section will provide support for a loan proposal, but the objective here is to give the reader, either you or your banker, a qualitative insight into the expected effect of the loan on the business.

Notice that Stefanie's Restaurant has asked that $5,000 be reserved as a line of credit to allow them to take advantage of opportunities that may arise in the future. Frequently a small business grows too fast, and when it turns to its bank for additional financing, the funds are denied. By reserving funds ahead of time, those funds will be available, but because they aren't disbursed, they won't incur additional interest expense. Stefanie's Restaurant is looking ahead to forestall cash-flow problems, a good example of careful planning.

Section One: The Business 51

I. Summary

The purpose of this section is to summarize the ideas you have developed in the preceding sections. This summary will help you make sure that the different parts of the analysis make sense, that they support each other logically and coherently, and that they will leave the reader with a concise, convincing statement that the project and plan are feasible.

A Sample Summary

Stefanie's Restaurant, Inc. is a full-menu, table service, casual restaurant located on Lake Delaney in Anytown, NY. It is of log cabin construction and is one of only two restaurants on Lake Delaney with docking facilities for boats. Stefanie Clark, the owner, is seeking a $25,000 loan to construct a 100-seat outdoor dining deck and additional rest rooms, and to purchase equipment and inventory to handle the additional seating.

Careful analysis of the market shows excess demand during the summer tourist and boating season that is not being met. Ms. Clark's formal education and practical, managerial experience in a number of restaurants assures that the expanded operation will be carefully controlled, competently managed, and will complement the advice of a thoughtfully selected advisory board.

The addition to the building will enable Stefanie's Restaurant to substantially increase its sales by meeting excess demand while maintaining profitability.

Guidelines for the Summary Section

The following checklist will help you make sure that important points are covered in your summary. These guidelines are a suggestion; your business plan may need to emphasize different points. If so, make sure that they are included.

Description of Business
    1. Business form: proprietorship, partnership, or corporation?
    2. Type of restaurant: gourmet, theme, casual table service, fast-food, cafeteria?
    3. What is the type of food and service?
    4. Is it a new restaurant? A takeover? An expansion?
    5. Why will your restaurant be profitable?
    6. What are your hours of service?
    7. Is it a seasonal operation?
    8. What have you learned about your type of restaurant from outside sources (trade suppliers, bankers, other business owners, publications)?

Product/Service
    1. What is your menu?
    2. What type of service are you offering?
    3. Which products are rising stars? Which are steady cash cows? Which are in decline or are investments in ego?
    4. What differentiates your restaurant from the competition?

The Market
    1. Who are your customers? Define your target markets.
    2. Are your markets growing, steady or declining?
    3. Is your market share growing, steady, or declining?
    4. Have you segmented your markets? How?
    5. Are your markets large enough for expansion?
    6. How will you attract, hold and increase your market share?
    7. Are you planning to enter or leave any markets?
    8. How do you price your products?

Location of Business
    1. Where are you located?
    2. Why is it a desirable area? A desirable building?
    3. What kind of space do you need?
    4. Are any demographic or other market shifts going on?

Competition
    1. Who are your nearest direct competitors?
    2. Who are your indirect competitors?
    3. How are their restaurants similar to and different from yours?
    4. What have you learned from their operations? From their advertising?

Section One: The Business

Management

1. How does your background/business experience help you in this business? For your own use, what weaknesses do you have and how will you compensate for them? What related work experience do you have?
2. Who is on the management team?
3. What are their strengths and weaknesses?
4. What are their duties?
5. Are these duties clearly defined? How?
6. What additional resources are available to your business?

Personnel

1. What are your current personnel needs?
2. What skills will your employees need in the near future? In five years?
3. What are your plans for hiring and training personnel?

Application and Expected Effect of Loan (Investment)

1. How will the loan (investment) make your restaurant more profitable?
2. Should you buy or lease (equipment, your place of business, and so on)?
3. Do you need this money? Establish a procedure for making borrowing decisions, and plan your borrowing.

Section Two: Financial Data

Policy and control are the key ingredients of any successful business. Policy establishes what your business will do. Control measures the accomplishment of policy goals.

The heart of the operation is in the accounting system. Before you start your business, it is essential that you have a competent accountant set up a system to give you adequate accounting records according to the *Uniform System of Accounts for Restaurants*. (See *Uniform System of Accounts for Restaurants*, sixth edition, National Restaurant Association, 1990.) If you can't afford this, you are simply too undercapitalized to be in business. If you don't understand the need for accounting records, you don't have enough management experience to be starting a business. This is a common problem area for many small restaurants.

Control is essential. If you don't control your restaurant, it will control you.

The overriding policy of your restaurant is:
- to find out what your markets want,
- satisfy those wants, and
- make a profit while doing so.

The implementation of your policy depends on planning and using your plan as a means of controlling your restaurant. The first step toward managing your restaurant for profits is to establish a bookkeeping system that provides you with the raw data for the five control documents (balance sheet, break-even analysis, income statement, cash flow, and deviation analysis) that will be developed in this section.

Your bookkeeping system should be simple enough for you or an employee to keep up-to-date on a daily basis with provisions made for weekly, monthly, quarterly, and yearly summaries. The system must contain cash controls (a checkbook and a cash register tape are part of your bookkeeping system). Beyond this, your method of bookkeeping should be suited to your specific needs.

Since your bookkeeping system is the basis of your business information (control) system, it should follow the format in the *Uniform System of Accounts for Restaurants*. The system offers two principal

If you don't control your restaurant, it will control you.

benefits. First, it has been designed to provide the information needed to properly control a restaurant operation. Second, using the system will allow you to compare your operating results directly with industry standards.

There are three resources for setting up your bookkeeping system:
1. You or an in-house bookkeeper;
2. Business service firms;
3. Accountants.

Each has advantages and drawbacks. You should decide which suits your needs best. The do-it-yourself systems are lowest in cost but require more time and often provide less information than professional business service firms and accountants. However, business service firms and accountants cost considerably more. Your best bet is to check out all three before making your decision. Keep in mind that business service firms and accountants act as outside staff (management consultants) for your business as part of their services. This extra service alone often justifies their higher costs.

The kinds of insights a good accountant, whether with a business service firm or a CPA firm (Certified Public Accountant), can bring, include analysis and interpretation of your financial statements, wide experience with many other small businesses, knowledge about people and markets that can help you, advice on choosing and using up-to-date computer power, and other general managerial tools. They also provide tax advice, which should be the least of your worries. (Sometimes a good tax accountant can actually make you more money in tax savings than he or she costs in fees.)

Develop your financial statements with an eye on your information needs.

The five control documents mentioned earlier provide the structure for your planning efforts. Properly used, they act as a budgeting tool, an early warning system, a problem identifier, and a solution generator. Used inconsistently or not at all, they are worthless. Used incorrectly they are dangerous. Misleading financial information can lead to making bad or disastrous decisions.

These documents needn't be very complicated. Develop your financial statements with an eye on your information needs, using your common sense and your accountant's experience as guides to the level of detail needed. (It's also possible to suffer from too much information.)

These statements should be used systematically. Make it policy to spend at least several hours (preferably free from distractions) each month checking them over once your business is underway. By doing so your information will be fresh and of greatest value to you, and help you plan profitable strategies, make good business decisions, and set reasonable objectives for the future.

Section Two: Financial Data

Ultimately, your accounting system should be a working model of your restaurant. A business manager has two concurrent objectives (which may conflict): to make a profit and to pay bills as they come due. These objectives are reflected in the two most important financial statements: the income statement and the cash flow projection. The income statement (also called the profit and loss statement) is designed to show how well the company's operations are performing over time by subtracting expenses from sales (profit or loss). The cash flow projection is designed to show how well the company is managing its cash (liquidity) by subtracting disbursements (actual cash outlays) from cash received.

The balance between profitability and liquidity can be hard to maintain. Fast growth (with high profits) can deplete cash, causing illiquidity. Companies have been known to fail even while they are profitable. The role of projected income and cash flow statements is to help you spot these kinds of severe problems in time to do something to forestall them such as raise new capital or arrange for the right kind of financing. Your banker will be helpful here—ask.

Companies have been known to fail even while they are profitable.

The break-even statement is based on the income and cash flow statements. Break-even analysis is a technique that no business can afford to ignore. Basically, the break-even statement shows the volume of revenue from sales you need to exactly balance the sum of your fixed and variable expenses. This document can be used in such critically important areas as setting prices, deciding whether to buy or lease equipment, projecting profits or losses at different sales volumes, and even determining whether to hire a new employee.

The balance sheet records the past effect of such decisions. More to the point, it records what the cash position (liquidity) of the business is and what the owner's equity is at a given point in time. These are directly affected by the cash flow and income statement, which are the records of how the business operates over time.

The deviation analysis compares actual performance to projected or budgeted performance on a monthly basis. As a guard against runaway expenses or destroyed budgets, it's unbeatable. You should compare both income statement and cash flow projections against actual performance. Most business experts will agree that more businesses are destroyed by the cumulative effects of a lot of small, sloppy errors (which deviation analysis highlights and helps you correct) than by large, powerful, obvious mismanagement.

Together, the income statement, cash flow, break-even, deviation analysis and balance sheet affords a comprehensive model of the operations, liquidity, and the past and near future of your restaurant. If you have a computer and spreadsheet software, the information can be easily manipulated to give you answers to many revealing what-if questions: What if we raised prices five percent? What if we lose 15 percent of our customer base? Would it make sense to add these fixed expenses to obtain ten percent greater productivity? And so on.

The value of such an interactive model of your business is hard to overstate. If you are not familiar with computerized financial models, check with the nearest business school (or your accountant). Just being able to trace out the short-term financial implications of a business decision can make a big difference in the quality of your judgments, to say nothing of your profits.

If there is only a single statement that is available, let it be your cash flow. A business that can't pay its bills can't stay in business for long even though the business may be operating at a profit. A schematic model of the cash flow is shown on page 83. Remember: Cash inflows must be greater than or equal to cash outflows.

Projections are an integral part of the Financial Data section, and are critical to accurately evaluating the feasibility of your deal and to planning just how large an investment is required to get your business to a stable level of operation. Your assumptions must be carefully thought out and explained. Be honest here for your own benefit: Over-optimism can accelerate failure.

The following items should appear in the Financial Data section:
- A. Sources and Applications of Funding
- B. Capital Equipment List
- C. Balance Sheet
- D. Break-Even Analysis
- E. Income Statement Projections
- F. Cash Flow Projections
- G. Deviation Analysis
- H. Historical Records (for an existing business)

Section Two: Financial Data

A. Sources and Applications of Funding

This subsection is needed for financing proposals, but also is handy for you as the owner. It's a restatement of the information in Section One-H: Application and Expected Effect of Loan on page 48. Major anticipated expenditures should be supported by copies of contracts, lease or purchase agreements, or other relevant documents.

The information presented here will show up in the cash flow projections, as the timing of the funds' flow is particularly important to maintaining liquidity.

A Sample Description of Sources and Applications of Funding
Stefanie's Restaurant, Inc.

Source:	
1. Mortgage Loan	$22,000
2. Term Loan	3,000
3. New Investment from Stefanie Clark	10,000
Total	**$ 35,000**

Applications	
1. Renovations (Dining Deck and Rest Rooms)	$ 22,000
2. Furniture, Fixtures, and Equipment	6,500
3. Inventories	1,500
4. Cash Reserve for Contingencies	5,000
Total	**$ 35,000**

To be secured by the assets of the business and a personal guarantee of the principal, Stefanie Clark.

B. Capital Equipment List

Your business plan should contain a capital equipment list to help maintain control over depreciable assets, for insurance purposes, to ensure against letting your reserve for replacement of capital equipment become too low (or be used as a slush fund), and to assist in the creation of a cost budget.

Capital equipment is equipment that you use to store or prepare food and beverages, provide a service, or use to sell, store and deliver merchandise. It is not equipment that you will sell in the normal course of business, but rather is equipment that you will use and wear out or consume as you do business. This does not include items that are expected to need replacement annually or more frequently such as china, silverware and glasssware.

Examples of capital equipment are office furniture and business machines (desks, typewriters, computers, adding machines), store fixtures (display cases, refrigeration units, permanent fixtures such as air conditioning and lighting fixtures), tables, chairs and service stations, kitchen equipment and delivery vehicles. None of these types of equipment is expected to wear out before a period of years. These goods are depreciable. Depreciation, the writing off of fixed assets over a period of years, is expressed as "depreciation expense" on the income statement, and serves to shelter income against taxes so you can replace the equipment as needed.

A sample capital equipment list for Stefanie's Restaurant appears below. No allowance for depreciation has been made since it is a new business. Otherwise, a column for accumulated depreciation would be shown so the depreciated value of the capital equipment could be displayed.

Section Two: Financial Data

A Sample Capital Equipment List
Stefanie's Restaurant, Inc.

Major Equipment and Normal Accessories:	Model:	Cost or List Price (whichever is lower):
Panasonic Commercial Microwave Oven	NE1257	$862
Castle 6 Burner Range and Oven	C330	1,620
Cecilware Heavy Duty Fryer	ELT500	729
Univex Slicing Machine	QF071-7510	799
Delfield 2 Door Reach-in Refrigerator	6051S	2,115
Delfield 2 Door Reach-in Freezer	6151S	2,480
Amerikooler 8' x 8' Walk-in Cooler	8X8C	3,345
KaTom 30" x 8' Stainless Steel Work Table	A308	250
KaTom 30" x 4' Stainless Steel Work Table	A304	150
Polar 21" x 54" 3-Compartment Sink with Drainboard	21543164	656
Total Major Equipment		**$13,006**

Other Equipment		
Kitchen Utensils	various	$500
China, Silverware, Glassware	various	2,000
Safe	1879 Diebold Mosler	200
Cash Register	523NCR	350
Calculator	TI-120	65
Computer and Software	IBM XT	2,100
Restaurant Sign	custom	600
Total Other Equipment		**$5,815**

C. Balance Sheet

Balance sheets are designed to show how the assets, liabilities and net worth of a company are distributed at a given point in time. The format is standardized to facilitate analysis and comparison. Do not deviate from it.

Balance sheets for all companies contain the same categories arranged in the same order.

Balance sheets for all companies, great and small, contain the same categories arranged in the same order. The difference is one of detail. Your balance sheet should be designed with your business information needs in mind. These will differ according to the size of your restaurant and the amount of information that your bookkeeping and accounting systems make available.

A Sample Balance Sheet Format
>   Name of Business
>   Date (month, day, year)
>   Balance Sheet

Assets

Current Assets		$ _____
Fixed Assets	$ _____	
Less Accumulated Depreciation	$ _____	
Net Fixed Assets		$ _____
Other Assets		$ _____
Total Assets:		$ _____

Footnotes:

Liabilities

Current Liabilities	$ _____
Long-Term Liabilities	$ _____
Total Liabilities:	$ _____

Net Worth (total assets minus total liabilities) or

Owner's Equity	$ _____
Total Liabilities and Net Worth	$ _____

Footnotes:

The categories can be defined more precisely. However, the order of the categories is important and you should follow it. They are arranged in order of decreasing liquidity (for assets) and decreasing immediacy (for liabilities). A brief description of each principal category follows:

    1. Current Assets: cash, government securities, marketable securities, notes receivable (other than from officers or employees), accounts receivable, inventories, prepaid expenses, any other item that will or could be converted to cash in the normal course of business within one year.

2. Fixed Assets: land, buildings, equipment, leasehold improvements, other items that have an expected useful business life measured in years. Depreciation is applied to those fixed assets that, unlike land, will wear out. The fixed asset value of a depreciable item is shown as the net result of cost minus accumulated depreciation.

3. Other Assets: intangible assets such as goodwill, notes receivable from officers and employees, deferred charges such as pre-opening expenses, cost of liquor license, deposit on franchise or royalty contract.

4. Current Liabilities: accounts payable, notes payable, accrued expenses (wages, salaries, withholding tax, FICA), taxes payable, current portion of long-term debt, other obligations coming due within one year.

5. Long-Term Liabilities: mortgages, trust deeds, intermediate and long-term bank loans, equipment loans (all of these net of the current portion of long-term debt, which appears as a current liability).

6. Net Worth: owner's equity, retained earnings, other equity.

7. Footnotes: You should provide displays of any extraordinary item (for example, a schedule of payables). Contingent liabilities such as pending lawsuits should be included in the footnotes. Changes of accounting practices would also be mentioned here.

If you need to provide more detail, do so—but remember to follow the standard format. If your balance sheet is assembled by an accountant, the accountant will specify whether it is done with or without audit. If you do it yourself, it is without audit. The decision to use a CPA (Certified Public Accountant) should be made carefully for tax and other legal reasons.

A sample balance sheet for Stefanie's Restaurant follows on the next page.

The categories are arranged in order of decreasing liquidity (for assets) and decreasing immediacy (for liabilities).

The balance sheet for Stefanie's Restaurant is modestly detailed. No depreciation has been taken, for example, because the business has just been started. The Net Worth section could have been more complex. The important thing to notice is that it provides a level of detail appropriate for the purposes of the principals, who own all of the stock.

Some financing sources (banks or other investors) may want to see balance sheets projected for each quarter for the first year of operation and annually for the next two. This would quickly show changes in debt, net worth, and the general condition of the restaurant, and could be another helpful control document. You may wish to have a monthly balance sheet (easily done with a microcomputer-powered accounting system), but for many businesses, a year-end balance sheet is all that is required.

The balance sheet for Stefanie's Restaurant provides a level of detail appropriate for the purposes of the principals who own all of the stock.

Stefanie's Restaurant, Inc.
December 31, 19___

Balance Sheet

Assets

Current Assets:
Cash on Hand	$100	
Cash in Banks	2,387	
Food Inventory	2,350	
Beverage Inventory	620	
Supplies Inventory	200	
Prepaid Expenses	420	
Total Current Assets		$6,077

Fixed Assets:
Leasehold Improvements	$18,000		
Less: Accumulated Depreciation	1,428	16,572	
Furniture, Fixtures, Equipment	$16,321		
Less: Accumulated Depreciation	3,264	13,057	
China, Silver, Glassware		2,000	
Kitchen Utensils		500	
Net Book Value Fixed Assets		$32,129	

Other Assets:
Cost of Liquor License	1,400

TOTAL ASSETS: $39,606

Liabilities

Current Liabilities:
Accounts Payable	$3,580	
Payroll Taxes Payable	640	
Current Portion, Long-Term Debt	2,000	
Total Current Liabilities		$6,220

Long-Term Liabilities:
Note Payable (a)	$9,000	
Note Payable (b)	4,000	
Total Long-Term Liabilities		$13,000

TOTAL LIABILITIES $19,220

Net Worth

Stockholders' Equity
Capital Contribution	$20,000	
Retained Earnings	386	
Total Stockholders' Equity		$20,386

TOTAL LIABILITIES & STOCKHOLDERS' EQUITY $39,606

Accounts Payable Display:
Wholesale Food Supply	$3,380
Anytown Bakers	120
FVR Restaurant Supply	80
Total	$3,580

(a) Stefanie Clark's parents
(b) Maguire's Used Restaurant Equipment

Preliminary Balance Sheet Analysis

1. Working Capital. Working capital is calculated by subtracting current liabilities from current assets. Cash is only a portion of working capital. Stefanie's Restaurant's working capital is negative [$6,077–$6,220 = ($143)], a dangerous but not uncommon position for many small (and at times, large) restaurants to be in.

A low or negative working capital position is a major danger signal. A firm with this working capital situation is said to be illiquid. Because owners' equity is less than the debt, the creditors in effect "own" the business, and bankers would be reluctant to extend further loans. Among possible solutions to this type of problem would be a working capital loan (long-term, to be repaid from operating profits), sale of fixed assets, or financing accounts payable by arranging to spread payment over a longer term. The best solution is to get new equity investment. (See sources and applications section on page 90.)

2. Comparison. Comparison of year-end balance sheets over a period of years will highlight trends and spotlight weak areas. Since Stefanie's Restaurant is new, this option is not open to them. However, they can compare their restaurant to other, similar operations by ratio analysis.

3. Ratio Analysis. This technique permits comparison in terms of percentages rather than dollars, thus making comparisons with other restaurants more accurate and informative. Among the more useful ratios are:

A. Current Ratio. This measures the liquidity of the company, its ability to meet current obligations (those coming due during the current year). It is calculated by dividing current assets by current liabilities. For Stefanie's Restaurant, divide $6,077 by $6,220. This yields a current ratio of 0.98, which is well below the current ratio of 2.0 some analysts would like to see. Stefanie's Restaurant is mildly illiquid. However, you need to know exactly what is represented by the figures to make a meaningful analysis. Inventory composition, quality of receivables, time of year and position in the sales cycle are all possible factors affecting the current ratio.

B. Acid Test. This is another measure of liquidity (sometimes called the Quick Ratio), and it is calculated by dividing the most liquid assets (cash, securities and possibly current accounts receivable) by current liabilities. For Stefanie's Restaurant, $2,487 ÷ $6,220 = 0.40. The rule-of-thumb ratio should be 1.0.

A word of caution: The rule-of-thumb ratios are far from infallible, since the date on which the balance sheet is drawn and the kind of business will affect the ratios you come up with. Some companies need a current ratio of 2.7 to be considered liquid, others can get by with 1.5 or less (such as department stores just prior to the Christmas rush when their inventories and payables are particularly high).

To get trade figures for your restaurant, try the following:

- The National Restaurant Association and state and local restaurant associations.
- Annual statement studies, which your banker will usually have, available from the Robert Morris Associates.
- A friendly competitor, perhaps in a non-competing location.
- Your banker and accountant.

D. Break-Even Analysis

A break-even analysis provides a sales objective expressed in either dollar or unit sales at which your business will be breaking even, that is, neither making a profit nor losing money. Once you know your break-even point, you have an objective target that you can plan to reach by carefully reasoned steps.

It is essential to remember that: Increased sales do not necessarily mean increased profits.

More than one company has gone broke by ignoring the need for break-even analysis, especially in those cases where variable costs (those directly related to sales levels) get out of hand as sales volume grows.

Calculating the break-even point for a restaurant is relatively simple. Some of the figures you will need to calculate will have to be estimates. It is a good idea to make your estimates conservative by using somewhat pessimistic sales and margin figures, and by slightly overstating your expected costs.

The basic break-even formula is:

S = FC + VC
where
S = Break-even level of sales in dollars,
FC = Fixed costs in dollars, and
VC = Variable costs in dollars.

Fixed costs are those costs that remain constant no matter what your sales volume may be,[1] those costs that must be met even if you make no sales at all. These include overhead costs (rent, office and administrative costs, salaries, benefits, FICA, etc.) and "hidden costs" such as depreciation, amortization and interest.

Variable costs are those costs associated with sales including cost of goods sold, variable labor costs, and credit card or other commissions. These cost figures are further elaborated on in the next section, Income Projections.

When you want to calculate a projected break-even point and you therefore do not know what your total variable costs will be, you have

Increased sales do not necessarily mean increased profits.

---

[1] These costs remain constant only in a relevant range. Your sales could rise dramatically causing you to need a new building, some new administrative employees and new equipment that could drive your fixed costs up disproportionately. Fixed costs tend to move up in chunks, not smoothly, if sales rise quickly.

to use a variation of the basic "S = FC + VC" formula. If you know what gross margin (profit on sales) to expect as a percent of sales, use the following formula:

S = FC ÷ GM
where GM = Gross margin expressed as a percentage of sales

If instead of calculating a dollar break-even you want to determine how many customers you need to break even, simply divide the break-even point derived above in dollars by the average check to get the number of required customers.

A Sample Break-Even Analysis
Figures from Stefanie's Restaurant Income Statement for Year One (on page 76).

Fixed costs[2] FC	= $167,923	
Gross Margin	GM	= (182,709 ÷ 309,432) = 59%
Thus, break-even sales		= S = FC ÷ GM
		= ($167,923 ÷ .59)
		= $284,615/year
On a monthly basis, S		= $23,718/month

[2]*For the purposes of this example, all expenses other than cost of goods sold are considered "fixed." A more accurate analysis would result from breaking down the other expenses into "fixed" and "variable" portions.*

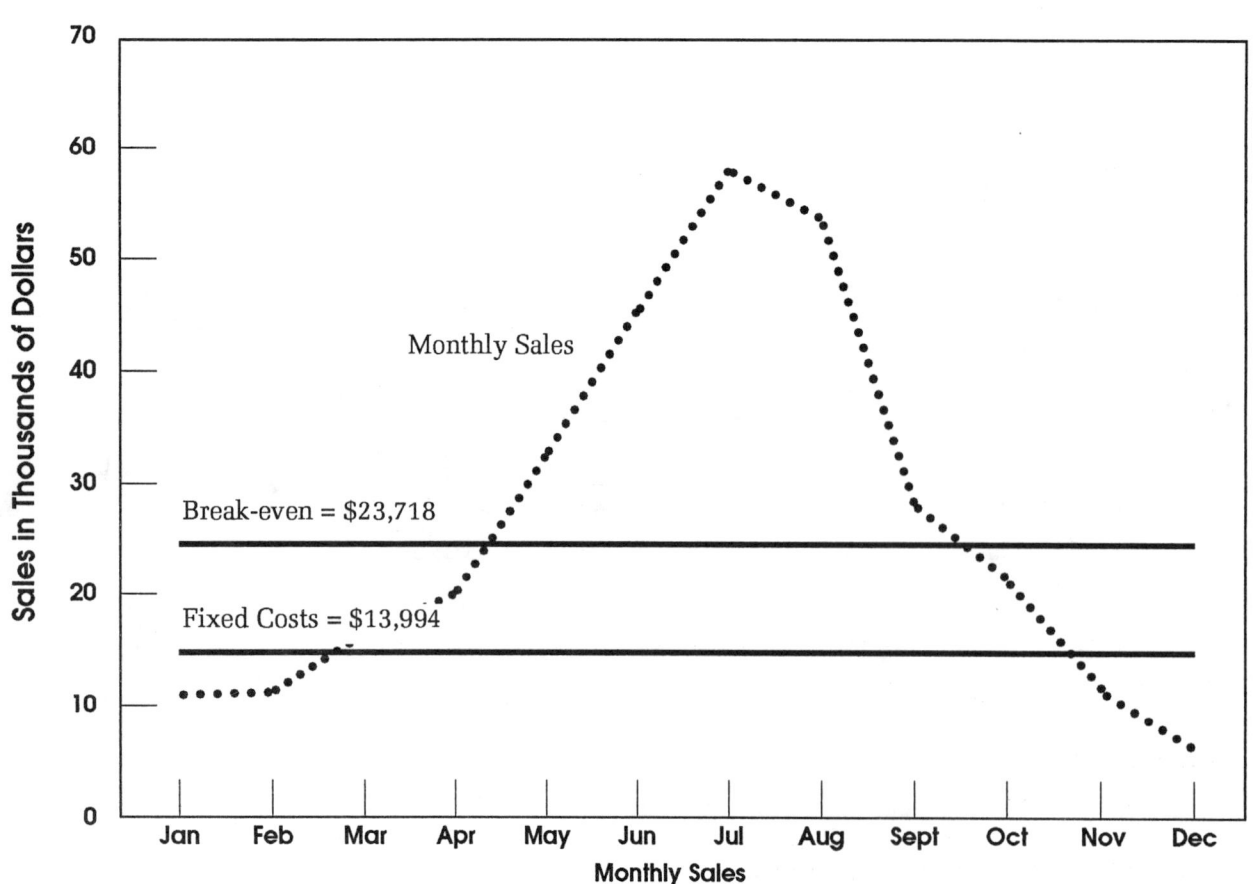

Monthly Sales

Section Two: Financial Data

This pictorial representation of break-even points is a handy way to make objectives more tangible than the usual "$24,000 a month" kind of goal. It can be very illuminating (or daunting) to post your break-even projections, tracing in some vivid color how near the projections you have come.

You can also use break-even charts to measure progress toward annual profit goals. Suppose Stefanie's Restaurant had aimed at a $25,000 profit the first year. What sales would be needed?

$$S = (FC + Profit) \div GM$$
where Profit = $25,000;
$$S = (\$167,923 + 25,000) \div 0.59$$
$$= (\$193,923) \div 0.59 = \$326,988/year$$
or $27,249/month.

Graphically,

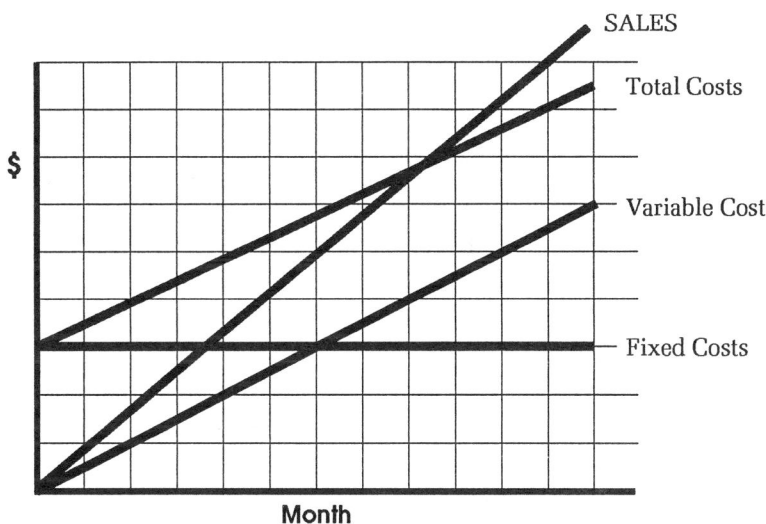

Any time you can help your employees visualize progress toward a goal, you benefit. Break-even charts (again) are useful for more than financial planning purposes. Once you have calculated break-even sales, you may find it very helpful to break the sales down in terms of customers needed. Used as a reality check, this can keep you from making overly optimistic projections. If you have a 100-seat restaurant and you need 500 covers per day to break even, chances are good you will not reach your goal.

Here is how Stefanie's Restaurant determined the number of customers needed per month to break-even:

Assumptions:
1. They assumed an average check of $10.00 per person.
2. Break-even in sales = $284,615
   or 28,462 customers per year
   or 2,372 customers per month

or 79 customers per day assuming seven days per week of operations.

Since Stefanie's Restaurant is an 80-seat restaurant, this means that they will have to average 79 meals per day or 1.0 "turns" per day to break even. This compares with National Restaurant Association figures of 128 meals per day or 1.6 turns per day for similar 80-seat restaurants.

Another way of looking at the break-even information is to compute sales per seat to break even: $284,615 (total annual break-even sales) ÷ 80 (number of seats available) = $3,558 (break-even sales per available seat). National Restaurant Association figures show a median sales per seat figure of $5,197 (and a lower quartile figure of $3,381) for 80-seat restaurants. Thus, Stefanie's Restaurant's break-even sales volume is relatively low compared to national averages.

Break-even analysis may also be represented pictorially. The diagramming helps establish forecasts, budgets and projections. Using a chart lets you substitute different combinations of numbers to obtain a rough estimate of their effect on your business.

A helpful technique is to make Worst Case, Best Case, and Most Probable Case assumptions, chart them to see how soon they cover fixed costs, and then derive more accurate figures by applying the various formulas and kinds of thinking displayed above. This is of particular value if you are thinking of making a capital investment and want a quick picture of the relative merits of buying or leasing.

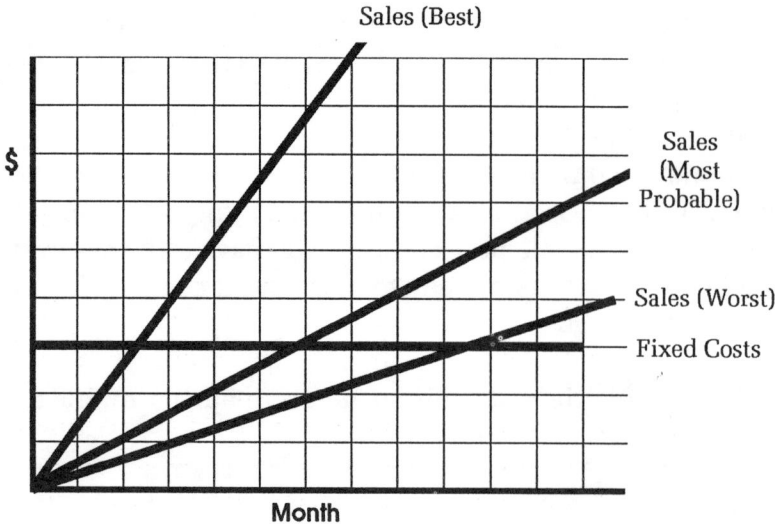

Section Two: Financial Data

E. Projected Income Statement

Income Statements, also called Profit and Loss Statements, complement balance sheets. The balance sheet gives a static picture of the company at a given point in time. The income statement provides a moving picture of the restaurant during a particular period of time.

Financial statements that depict a future period are called *pro forma* or projected financial statements. They represent what the company is expected to look like financially, based on a set of assumptions about the economy, market growth and other factors.

Income projections are forecasting and budgeting tools estimating income and anticipating expenses in the near-to-middle range future. For most businesses (and for most bankers) income projections covering one to three years are more than adequate. In some cases, a longer range projection may be called for, but in general, the longer the projection, the less accurate it will be as a guide to action.

Income projections are forecasting and budgeting tools.

You don't need a crystal ball to make your projection. While no set of projections will be 100 percent accurate, experience and practice tend to make the projections more precise. Even if your income projections are not accurate, they will provide you with a rough set of benchmarks to test your progress toward short-term goals. They become the base of your budgets.

There is nothing sacred about income projections. If they are wildly incorrect, correct them to make a more realistic guide. When you do this is a matter of judgment. A rule of thumb is that if they are more than 20 percent off for a quarter (three months), redo them. If they are less than 20 percent off, wait for another quarter. Do not change your projections more often. In a short period, certain trends will be magnified, and these distortions will usually be evened out over the long run. Of course, if you find you have omitted a major expense item or discover a significant new source of revenue, you will want to make immediate corrections. Use your common sense.

The reasoning behind income projection is: Since most expenses are predictable and income doesn't fluctuate too drastically, the future will be much like the past. For example, if your food cost has historically been 38 percent of net sales, it will (barring strong evidence to the contrary) continue to be 38 percent of net sales. If you are in a start-up situation, look for financial statement information and income ratios for restaurants similar to yours. The National Restaurant Association's *Restaurant Industry Operations Report 1991*, as well as local and state restaurant associations, are the sources you should contact. (See Appendix Three: Resources for Restaurateurs.)

It is important to be systematic and thorough when you list your expenses. The expense that bleeds your business dry (makes it illiquid) is almost always one that was overlooked or seriously misjudged and is therefore unplanned for. There are some expenses that cannot be foreseen, and the best way to allow for them is to be conservative in your estimates and to document your assumptions.

Try to understate your expected sales and overstate expenses.

It is better to exceed a conservative budget than to fall below optimistic projections. However, being too far under can also create problems—such as not having enough capital to finance growth. Basing income projections on hopes or unjustified fears is hazardous to your business's health. Be realistic; your budget is an extension of your forecasts.

Income statements and projections are standardized to facilitate comparison and analysis. They must be dated to indicate the period of time they cover and also contain notes to explain any unusual items such as windfall profits, litigation expenses and judgments, changes in depreciation schedules and other material information. Any assumptions should be footnoted—to help remind you of how the numbers were originally justified, and to provide a boost up the learning curve when you review your projections before making new ones.

Income statements should be reviewed at least once a quarter to check their validity and, if necessary, to make adjustments or make changes in your restaurant's operations. As a budget tool, the actual progress of your restaurant should be compared against the projections every month. You have to detect deviations as soon as possible to correct problems before they become major, and to seize opportunities while they are still fresh.

Suggested formats for an income statement and an income projection follow, and are based upon the *Uniform System of Accounts for Restaurants*.

Remember: The purpose of financial statements and forecasts is to provide you with the maximum amount of useful information and guidance, not to dazzle a prospective investor.

Explanation of Sample
Food Sales: Sales of food items and beverage items (e.g., coffee, tea, soft drinks) if the cost of such beverages is charged against food cost.

Beverage Sales: Sale of all beer, wine, liquor, and other alcoholic and nonalcoholic beverages whose cost is charged against beverage cost.

Detect deviations as soon as possible to correct problems before they become major, and seize opportunities while they are still fresh.

A Sample Income Statement Format
Using the *Uniform System of Accounts for Restaurants*

Sales
    Food Sales
    Beverage Sales
Total Sales

Cost of Sales
    Food
    Beverage
Total Cost of Sales

Gross Profit
    Other Income
Total Income

Controllable Expenses
    Payroll
    Employee Benefits
    Direct Operating Expenses
    Advertising and Promotion
    Utilities
    Administration and General
    Repairs and Maintenance
Total Controllable Expenses

Income Before Occupancy Costs

Occupancy Costs
    Rent
    Property Taxes
    Other Taxes
    Property Insurance
Total Occupancy Costs

Income Before Interest and Depreciation
    Interest
    Depreciation
    Restaurant Profit
    Other Deductions
    Income Before Taxes
    Taxes
Net Profit (Loss)

Cost of Sales, Food: The cost to the restaurant of the food that was available for sale to the customers. Calculated by using the formula (Beginning Inventory + Purchases – Ending Inventory = Cost of Goods Sold).

Cost of Sales, Beverages: The cost to the restaurant of the beverages which were available for sale to the customers. Calculated by using the formula (Beginning Inventory + Purchases — Ending Inventory = Cost of Good Sold).

Gross Profit: Total Sales less Total Cost of Sales.

Other Income: Income other than from food or beverage sales (e.g., banquet room rentals, gift shop items, vending machine commissions, etc.).

Total Income: Gross Profit plus Other Income.

Controllable Expenses: Operating expenses most directly influenced by the operating policy and management efficiency (see the *Uniform System of Accounts for Restaurants* for a complete explanation of the items and categories).

Occupancy Costs, Interest, Depreciation: Items that are relatively fixed based upon the financing structure of the restaurant and are not influenced by the day-to-day management decisions (see the *Uniform System of Accounts for Restaurants* for a complete explanation of the items).

The degree of pessimism you should build into a projection is a matter of judgment.

For the most useful projection, state your assumptions clearly. Do not put down numbers that you cannot rationally substantiate. Do not puff your gross sales projection to make the net profit positive. Give yourself conservative sales figures and pessimistic expense figures to make the success of your deal more probable. Be realistic. You want your projections to reflect the realities of your restaurant.

Income and Cash Flow Forecasting

Restaurants should make three-year projections for both planning purposes and loan proposals. The proper sequence for both income and cash flow projections is:

1. A three-year summary.
2. First year projected by month. If the restaurant doesn't break even in the first year, you might want to continue the monthly projections until it does.
3. Years two and three by quarter.

If you are already in business or are considering taking over an existing restaurant, historical financial statements should be included for two immediately previous years. Tax returns help to substantiate the validity of unaudited statements.

Section Two: Financial Data

A Note on Sales Forecasts

Whether you've been in operation for a while or are starting a restaurant, your sales forecasts are the basis for most of your financial planning.

One helpful technique to use involves breaking your projected sales into a three-column form to arrive at a "most likely" figure.

Begin by assuming the worst. In the column headed "low," put down the sales you expect if everything goes wrong—poor weather, loss of market share to a new competitor and so on. Be gloomy. Assume your waitstaff will be loutish, lazy and surly.

Then—this is more fun—assume everything works out the way you'd wish. In the column headed "high," put down your rosiest hopes. All your promotional efforts will succeed, markets will grow dynamically, your competition will stub their toes and slink away from the market, your restaurant will become the "in-spot."

Now look to a realistic scenario, where things work out in between the high and low estimates. The figures here will (usually) be more accurate than a one-time estimate can be, since more thought has gone into their preparation. Do this for the period you need to forecast.

Your sales forecasts are the basis for most of your financial planning.

Sales Forecast: For (month, year) to (month, year)

Sales:	Low	Most Likely	High
Draft beer			
Bottle beer			
Liquor			
Wine			
Nonalcoholic beverages			
Food			
Total Sales:			

You can apply the same process to forecasting expenses, even though most expenses are reasonably predictable once the sales forecasts have been established.

Explanation for Income Statement Projections

This section will:

    A. Explain how the figures on the projection were calculated.
    B. Detail the assumptions made.

    Food Sales and Beverage Sales: The ratio of food sales to beverage sales that actually occurred in year one was projected to remain the

Stefanie's Restaurant
Income Statement—By Month
Actual—Year One, Jan. 1 to Dec. 31, 19___

	JAN	FEB	MAR	APR	MAY	JUN	JUL	AUG	SEPT	OCT	NOV	DEC	Totals	%
Sales														
Food	7,558	7,904	11,057	14,111	25,108	34,759	46,670	44,520	22,892	15,288	7,832	4,255	241,954	78.2%
Beverage	2,959	2,978	4,129	4,066	7,095	10,701	12,220	10,638	5,643	3,999	2,076	974	67,478	21.8%
Total Sales	10,517	10,882	15,186	18,177	32,203	45,460	58,890	55,158	28,535	19,287	9,908	5,229	309,432	100.0%
Cost of Sales														
Food	5,185	4,625	5,179	6,128	10,701	12,963	17,899	16,519	9,747	5,824	5,198	2,765	102,733	42.5%
Beverage	922	1,430	1,701	1,944	2,387	3,374	4,148	3,948	2,039	1,557	712	879	25,041	37.1%
Total Cost of Sales	6,107	6,055	6,880	8,072	13,088	16,337	22,047	20,467	11,786	7,381	5,910	3,644	127,774	41.3%
Gross Profit	4,410	4,827	8,306	10,105	19,115	29,123	36,843	34,691	16,749	11,906	3,998	1,585	181,658	58.7%
Other Income	0	0	0	0	0	0	0	828	170	56	0	0	1,054	0.3%
Total Income	4,410	4,827	8,306	10,105	19,115	29,123	36,843	35,519	16,919	11,962	3,998	1,585	182,712	59.0%
Controllable Expenses														
Payroll	3,153	3,128	3,923	4,047	5,023	8,406	17,761	11,804	7,633	4,313	3,247	3,012	75,450	24.4%
Employee Benefits	369	982	554	853	422	2,093	1,907	1,372	665	1,056	1,062	115	11,450	3.7%
Direct Operating Exp.	488	384	1,121	878	1,481	2,757	1,589	1,988	404	1,685	340	361	13,476	4.4%
Advertising & Promotion	941	945	739	692	1,121	1,486	2,356	1,128	1,175	856	994	941	13,374	4.3%
Utilities	535	1,212	676	1,215	443	1,355	571	1,960	607	1,486	194	411	10,665	3.4%
Administrative & General	69	828	533	166	291	530	419	406	600	210	172	223	4,447	1.4%
Repairs & Maintenance	99	73	554	243	1,284	1,894	1,365	884	404	1,382	166	17	8,365	2.7%
Total Controllable Exp.	5,654	7,552	8,100	8,094	10,065	18,521	25,968	19,542	11,488	10,988	6,175	5,080	137,227	44.3%
Income Before Occupancy Costs	(1,244)	(2,725)	206	2,011	9,050	10,602	10,875	15,977	5,431	974	(2,177)	(3,495)	45,485	14.7%
Occupancy Costs														
Rent	1,200	1,200	1,200	1,200	1,200	1,200	1,200	1,200	1,200	1,200	1,200	1,200	14,400	4.7%
Property Taxes	374	374	374	374	374	374	374	374	374	374	374	374	4,488	1.5%
Other Taxes														
Property Insurance	518	518	518	518	518	518	518	518	518	518	518	518	6,216	2.0%
Total Occupancy Costs	2,092	2,092	2,092	2,092	2,092	2,092	2,092	2,092	2,092	2,092	2,092	2,092	25,104	8.1%
Income Before Interest and Dep.	(3,336)	(4,817)	(1,886)	(81)	6,958	8,510	8,783	13,885	3,339	(1,118)	(4,269)	(5,587)	20,381	6.6%
Interest	75	75	75	75	75	75	75	75	75	75	75	75	900	0.3%
Depreciation	391	391	391	391	391	391	391	391	391	391	391	391	4,692	1.5%
Restaurant Profit	(3,802)	(5,283)	(2,352)	(547)	6,492	8,044	8,317	13,419	2,873	(1,584)	(4,735)	(6,053)	14,789	4.8%
Other Deductions														
Income Before Income Taxes	(3,802)	(5,283)	(2,352)	(547)	6,492	8,044	8,317	13,419	2,873	(1,584)	(4,735)	(6,053)	14,789	4.8%

Stefanie's Restaurant
Income Projection—By Quarter
Year Two

	1st Quarter	2nd Quarter	3rd Quarter	4th Quarter	Total	Percent
Sales						
Food	29,171	81,375	125,490	30,112	266,148	78.2%
Beverage	11,073	24,048	31,351	7,752	74,224	21.8%
Total Sales	40,244	105,423	156,841	37,864	340,372	100.0%
Cost of Sales						
Food	12,386	34,552	53,283	12,786	113,007	42.5%
Beverage	4,109	8,924	11,635	2,877	27,545	37.1%
Total Cost of Sales	16,495	43,476	64,918	15,663	140,552	41.3%
Gross Profit	23,749	61,947	91,923	22,201	199,820	58.7%
Other Income	300	300	300	300	1,200	0.4%
Total Income	24,049	62,247	92,223	22,501	201,020	59.1%
Controllable Expenses						
Payroll	11,224	19,224	40,918	11,629	82,995	24.4%
Employee Benefits	2,096	3,705	4,338	2,456	12,595	3.7%
Direct Operating Exp.	2,192	5,628	4,379	2,625	14,824	4.4%
Advertising & Promotion	2,888	3,629	5,125	3,070	14,712	4.3%
Utilities	2,665	3,314	3,452	2,300	11,731	3.4%
Administrative & General	1,573	1,086	1,568	666	4,893	1.4%
Repairs & Maintenance	799	3,763	2,918	1,722	9,202	2.7%
Total Controllable Exp.	23,437	40,349	62,698	24,468	150,952	44.3%
Income Before Occupancy Costs	612	21,898	29,525	(1,967)	50,068	14.7%
Occupancy Costs						0.0%
Rent	3,600	3,600	3,600	3,600	14,400	4.2%
Property Taxes	1,234	1,234	1,234	1,234	4,936	1.5%
Other Taxes	0	0	0	0	0	0.0%
Property Insurance	1,709	1,709	1,709	1,709	6,836	2.0%
Total Occupancy Costs	6,543	6,543	6,543	6,543	26,172	7.7%
Income Before Interest and Dep.	(5,931)	15,355	22,982	(8,510)	23,896	7.0%
Interest	225	225	225	225	900	0.3%
Depreciation	1,173	1,173	1,173	1,173	4,692	1.4%
Restaurant Profit	(7,329)	13,957	21,584	(9,908)	18,304	5.4%
Other Deductions	0	0	0	0	0	0.0%
Income Before Income Taxes	(7,329)	13,957	21,584	(9,908)	18,304	5.4%

Stefanie's Restaurant
Income Projection—By Quarter
Year Three

	1st Quarter	2nd Quarter	3rd Quarter	4th Quarter	Total	Percent
Sales						
Food	32,088	89,512	138,039	33,123	292,762	78.2%
Beverage	12,180	26,452	34,486	8,528	81,646	21.8%
Total Sales	44,268	115,964	172,525	41,651	374,408	100.0%
Cost of Sales						
Food	12,193	34,015	52,455	12,587	111,250	38.0%
Beverage	3,898	8,465	11,036	2,729	26,128	32.0%
Total Cost of Sales	16,091	42,480	63,491	15,316	137,378	36.7%
Gross Profit	28,177	73,484	109,034	26,335	237,030	63.3%
Other Income	300	300	300	300	1,200	0.3%
Total Income	28,477	73,784	109,334	26,635	238,230	63.6%
Controllable Expenses						
Payroll	12,347	21,146	45,010	12,792	91,295	24.4%
Employee Benefits	2,305	4,075	4,772	2,702	13,854	3.7%
Direct Operating Exp.	2,412	6,190	4,817	2,887	16,306	4.4%
Advertising & Promotion	3,176	3,992	5,637	3,377	16,182	4.3%
Utilities	2,932	3,646	3,797	2,530	12,905	3.4%
Administrative & General	1,730	1,194	1,724	732	5,380	1.4%
Repairs & Maintenance	878	4,139	3,210	1,894	10,121	2.7%
Total Controllable Exp.	25,780	44,382	68,967	26,914	166,043	44.3%
Income Before Occupancy Costs	2,697	29,402	40,367	(279)	72,187	19.3%
Occupancy Costs						
Rent	3,600	3,600	3,600	3,600	14,400	3.8%
Property Taxes	1,358	1,358	1,358	1,358	5,432	1.5%
Other Taxes	0	0	0	0	0	0.0%
Property Insurance	1,880	1,880	1,880	1,880	7,520	2.0%
Total Occupancy Costs	6,838	6,838	6,838	6,838	27,352	7.3%
Income Before Interest and Dep.	(4,141)	22,564	33,529	(7,117)	44,835	12.0%
Interest	225	225	225	225	900	0.2%
Depreciation	1,173	1,173	1,173	1,173	4,692	1.3%
Restaurant Profit	(5,539)	21,166	32,131	(8,515)	39,243	10.5%
Other Deductions	0	0	0	0	0	0.0%
Income Before Income Taxes	(5,539)	21,166	32,131	(8,515)	39,243	10.5%

Stefanie's Restaurant
Income Projection
Three Year Summary

	Year One	Year Two	Year Three
Sales			
Food	241,954	266,148	292,762
Beverage	67,478	74,224	81,646
Total Sales	309,432	340,372	374,408
Cost of Sales			
Food	102,733	113,007	111,250
Beverage	25,041	27,545	26,128
Total Cost of Sales	127,774	140,552	137,378
Gross Profit	181,658	199,820	237,030
Other Income	1,054	1,200	1,200
Total Income	182,712	201,020	238,230
Controllable Expenses			
Payroll	75,450	82,995	91,295
Employee Benefits	11,450	12,595	13,854
Direct Operating Exp.	13,476	14,824	16,306
Advertising & Promotion	13,374	14,712	16,182
Utilities	10,665	11,731	12,905
Administrative & General	4,447	4,893	5,380
Repairs & Maintenance	8,365	9,202	10,121
Total Controllable Exp.	137,227	150,952	166,043
Income Before Occupancy Costs	45,485	50,068	72,187
Occupancy Costs			
Rent	14,400	14,400	14,400
Property Taxes	4,488	4,936	5,432
Other Taxes	0	0	0
Property Insurance	6,216	6,836	7,520
Total Occupancy Costs	25,104	26,172	27,352
Income Before Interest and Dep.	20,381	23,896	44,835
Interest	900	900	900
Depreciation	4,692	4,692	4,692
Restaurant Profit	14,789	18,304	39,243
Other Deductions	0	0	0
Income Before Income Taxes	14,789	18,304	39,243

same in years two and three. The dollar amount of food and beverage sales was forecast to increase ten percent each year.

Cost of Sales, Food and Beverage: The cost of food sales and the cost of beverage sales were forecast to remain at the same percentage (42.5 percent and 37.1 percent respectively) for year two as was actually obtained in year one. Although this percentage is higher than Stefanie's Restaurant computed in the pricing section and higher than the national average (as shown in the section on deviation analysis), the same percentage was used due to the seasonal nature of the restaurant, which makes controlling costs more difficult in the slow seasons, and due to the fact that the owner wished to remain conservative in projecting income during the expansion in the second year. For the third year, the food cost percentage was projected to be lowered to 38 percent and the beverage cost percentage was projected to be lowered to 32 percent—both of which more closely resemble national averages. The reason for lowering the forecasted cost percentages in the third year was because the owner felt she would then have more time to manage costs since the business cycle should have stabilized somewhat.

Gross Profit: Total Sales less Total Cost of Sales.

Other Income: Estimated to remain fairly constant since the restaurant is small and does not have the room to expand offering of products other than food and beverage.

Total Income: Gross Profit plus Other Income

Controllable Expenses: All operating expenses were estimated to increase ten percent in year two and an additional ten percent in year three. Although these increases may seem high, Stefanie's Restaurant wished to remain conservative when projecting the income statement. The payroll cost is lower than the national average, but this is due to the fact that the owner is working daily in the business and taking a minimal salary. The owner does not expect to take more than a minimal salary ($1,200 per month) to enable the business to accumulate capital and fund expansion.

Occupancy Costs, Interest, Depreciation: Rent is not projected to increase because the landlord has agreed to a three-year lease with no increases since Stefanie's Restaurant is paying for all the leasehold improvements. Property taxes and property insurance are both projected to increase at a rate of ten percent each year. Interest and depreciation figures will remain constant unless the expansion is undertaken, in which case interest should increase by approximately $2,250 ($25,000 @ 9 percent interest) and depreciation will increase by approximately $4,800.

Stefanie's Restaurant does not expect to make much money for the first few years. This is no surprise for a business so thinly capitalized.

Information is the most valuable result of financial statements. Accurate, timely information helps you run your business.

Information is the most valuable result of financial statements.

Section Two: Financial Data

F. Cash Flow Projection

The cash flow projection is the most important financial planning tool available to you. If you were limited to one financial statement (which fortunately isn't the case), the cash flow projection would be the one to choose.

For a new or growing restaurant, the cash flow projection can make the difference between success and failure. For an ongoing restaurant, it can make the difference between growth and stagnation.

Your cash flow analysis will:
1. Show you how much cash your business will need;
2. When it will be needed;
3. Whether you should look for equity, debt, operating profits, or sale of fixed assets; and
4. Where the cash will come from.

The cash flow projection attempts to budget the cash needs of a business and shows how cash will flow in and out of the business over a stated period of time. Cash flows into the restaurant business from sales, collection of receivables, capital injections, etc., and flows out through cash payments for expenses of all kinds.

This financial tool emphasizes the points in your calendar when money will be coming into and going out of your restaurant. The advantage of knowing when cash outlays must be made is the ability to plan for those outlays and not be forced to resort to unexpected borrowing to meet cash needs. Illiquidity is a killer, even for profitable restaurants. Lack of profits won't kill a restaurant (noncash expenses such as depreciation can make your profits look negative, while your cash flow is positive). Lack of cash to meet your trade and other payables will.

If you project your cash flow for the near to intermediate future, you can see the effect of a loan to your restaurant far more clearly than from the income statement. You may be able to find ways to finance your restaurant operation or minimize your credit needs to keep interest expense down. Many of the advantages of studying the cash flow projection stem from timing: More options are available to you, at lower costs, with less panic.

Cash is generated primarily by sales, and most restaurant sales are cash. Customers expect to pay cash (or use credit cards, which are instantly converted to cash). However, not all sales are cash sales. Perhaps your business is all cash—but if you offer any credit (charge accounts for individuals or companies) to your customers, you need to have a means of telling when those credit sales will turn into cash-in-

The cash flow projection can make the difference between success and failure, and between growth and stagnation.

hand. This is blurred in the income statement, but made very clear by the cash flow. Your restaurant may be subject to seasonal bills, and again, a cash flow makes the liquidity problems attending such large, occasional expenses clear.

A cash flow deals only with actual cash transactions. Depreciation, a noncash expense, does not appear on a cash flow. Loan repayments (including interest), on the other hand, do, since they represent a cash disbursement.

After it has been developed, use your cash flow projection as a budget. If the cash outlays for a given item increase over the amount allotted for a given month, you should find out why and take corrective action as soon as possible. If the figure is lower, you should also find out why. If the cash outlay is lower than expected, it is not necessarily a good sign. Maybe a bill wasn't paid. By reviewing the movement of your cash position you can better control your restaurant.

On a more positive note, the savings may tip you off to a new way of economizing. Discrepancies between expected and actual cash flows are indicators of opportunities as well as problems. If the sales figures don't match the cash flow projections, look for the cause. Maybe projections were too low. Maybe you've opened a new market or introduced a new product that can be pushed even harder.

Use the Cash Flow Sketch on the next page to make sure you don't omit any ordinary cash flow item. But be sure to add any items that are peculiar to your operation.

Cash flow projections lend themselves to computerization. Spreadsheet programs such as Lotus 1-2-3™ or Excel™ (among others) are made even more valuable because you can tie in graphic displays to your hard numbers, link together several different financial statements, or play "what-if" with much greater speed and accuracy than was possible when we were limited to pencils, adding machines, 13-column accounting paper and erasers.

Explanation of Year One Cash Flow Statement

The first year cash flow statement for Stefanie's Restaurant has been limited solely to cash flows as a result of operations in order to simplify some of the comparisons between cash flow from operations and profit or loss. The loans and investments made to Stefanie's Restaurant when it started in business would normally be shown as would the investment in fixed assets. When preparing initial cash flow projections for your restaurant, it is suggested that you compute cash flows from operations first (to see if the restaurant is going to generate enough cash to pay operating bills). Then go back and insert those items that have to do with financing the restaurant and purchasing

Section Two: Financial Data

Cash Flow Management Sketch

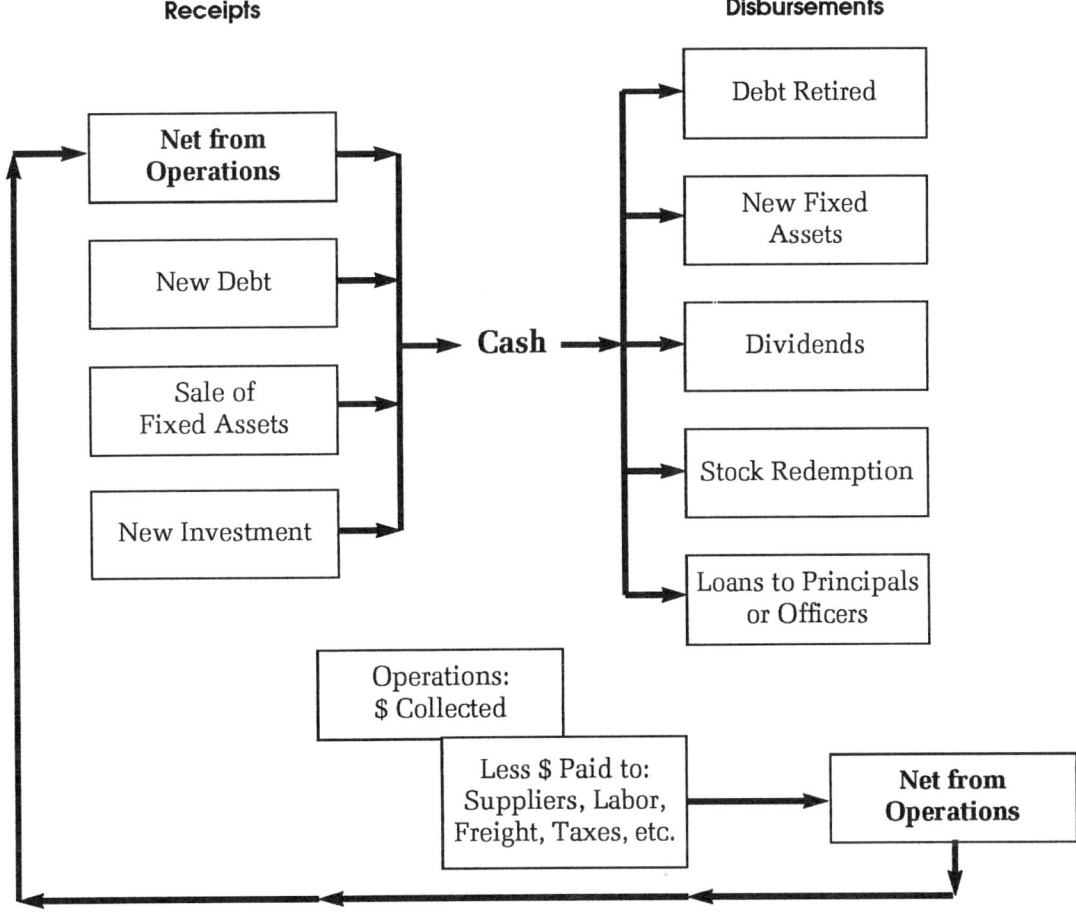

Cash Flow Sketch

1. Cash at Beginning of Period
   Add Revenues, etc.:
2. Sales of products (cash)
3. Sales of products (receivables collected)
4. Cash received from assets sold
5. Cash received from equity investment
6. Cash received from loans
7. Cash received from bad debt recovery
8. Miscellaneous cash received
   Total: Cash Received

   Subtract: Cash Disbursements
9. New inventory purchased for cash (food, beverage, supplies, other)
10. Salaries/wages
11. FICA, federal and state withholding tax
12. Fringe benefits paid
13. New equipment to be purchased for cash
    14. Kitchen equipment
    15. Furniture, fixtures
    16. China, silver, glass
17. Insurance premiums
18. Fees
    19. Accounting
    20. Legal
21. Utilities
    22. Telephone
    23. Heat, light, power
24. Advertising
25. Principal and interest on debt
26. Transportation
    27. Oil, gas
    28. Vehicle maintenance
    29. Tires
30. Music and entertainment
31. Provision for bad debts (if funded with cash)
32. Taxes payable
    33. Income (state, federal, other if applicable)
    34. Property
    35. Excise
    36. Sales taxes (if applicable)
37. Dividends paid, cash withdrawal by partner, or contribution to profit-sharing plan
38. Provision for unforeseen circumstances (if funded)
39. Provision for replacement of depreciable assets (if funded)

Total Cash Received less Total Disbursements Equals Cash at End of Period

Note: Only cash disbursements are included. These are actual dollars that you pay out, not obligations that you incur now to be paid off at some future date. Those appear on the income projection and balance sheet.

fixed assets as well as those items that indicate how debt will be repaid and dividends made to stockholders.

The first year cash flow statement is based on the assumption that all sales are in cash (credit card sales being considered the same as cash) and therefore there are no accounts receivable. If there were charge sales, then the cash receipts would be shown in the month they were actually received, not in the month that the sale was made.

The first year cash flow statement also assumes that all bills were paid immediately. If that were not the case, then cash disbursements would be shown in the month actually paid, not in the month when the expense was incurred.

A comparison of the first year income statement with the first year cash flow statement shows a profit of $14,786 and a cash flow of $19,478. The reason for this discrepancy ($4,692) is due to depreciation, which is a noncash expense and, therefore, is not taken into consideration on the cash flow statement.

A comparison of the two statements for the month of January shows a loss on the income statement of ($3,802) for January and a negative cash flow on the cash flow statement of ($5,804). The reason for this difference is due to the fact that expenses are allocated on the income statement to the month in which they are incurred, but they are shown on the cash flow statement in the month they are actually paid. Property taxes of $1,903 were paid in January but only $374 was allocated to the month. The same is true of the property insurance: the premium of $1,457 was paid in January but only $518 was allocated as an expense for the month. The income statement shows an interest expense of $75 for the month, but examination of the cash flow statement shows no interest payments were made until December. Finally, the income statement shows the depreciation expense of $391 in January, which, as already explained, is a noncash expense. The result of these items is that an excess of $2,002 in payments were made in January that were not allocated. The following table summarizes the results:

Section Two: Financial Data

Reconciliation of Cash Flow

Cash Disbursements:	
Property Taxes	$1,903
Property Insurance	1,457
Total Disbursements Made	$3,360

Expenses Allocated:	
Property Taxes	$374
Property Insurance	518
Interest	75
Depreciation	391
Total Expenses Allocated	1,358
Difference	$2,002
Summary	
Income (loss) from Income Statement	($3,802)
Disbursements Made but not Allocated	(2,002)
Cash Flow from Operations	($5,804)

Examination of the overall cash flow statement reveals that although Stefanie's Restaurant had a positive cash flow from operations of $19,478 for the year, the cash flow started out negative and reached as high as ($11,369) during the first four months before the operating results started to show a positive cash flow. Arrangements had to be made to cover the negative cash flow in the beginning of the year, and it is assumed that Stefanie Clark either loaned the business money from her savings or was able to arrange for a short-term loan from another source. One of the values of projected cash flow statements—as will be shown for the year two projections—is that the cash flow statement details exactly when cash loans are going to be needed because of business cycles and when such loans can be expected to be repaid.

A comparison of the two statements reveals other months when cash flows were different than profit or loss.

Explanation of Year Two Cash Flow Projections

The cash flow projections for year two show the impact of the loan Stefanie's Restaurant has applied for, the additional equity investment Stefanie Clark expects to make, and the disbursements involved with constructing the new dining deck and restrooms and purchasing the furniture, fixtures, and equipment.

The projection also reveals that—based upon expected operating

Stefanie's Restaurant
Cash Flow Statement—By Month
Actual—Year One, Jan. 1 to Dec. 31, 19___

	JAN	FEB	MAR	APR	MAY	JUN	JUL	AUG	SEPT	OCT	NOV	DEC	TOTALS
Cash Receipts													
Food Sales	7,558	7,904	11,057	14,111	25,108	34,759	46,670	44,520	22,892	15,288	7,832	4,255	241,954
Beverage Sales	2,959	2,978	4,129	4,066	7,095	10,701	12,220	10,638	5,643	3,999	2,076	974	67,478
Sales Receivables	0	0	0	0	0	0	0	0	0	0	0	0	0
Other Income	0	0	0	0	0	0	0	828	170	56	0	0	1,054
Total Cash Receipts	10,517	10,882	15,186	18,177	32,203	45,460	58,890	55,986	28,705	19,343	9,908	5,229	310,486
Cash Disbursements													
Cost of Sales, Food	5,185	4,625	5,179	6,128	10,701	12,963	17,899	16,519	9,747	5,824	5,198	2,765	102,733
Cost of Sales, Beverages	922	1,430	1,701	1,944	2,387	3,374	4,148	3,948	2,039	1,557	712	879	25,041
Controllable Expenses													0
Payroll	3,153	3,128	3,923	4,047	5,023	8,406	17,761	11,804	7,633	4,313	3,247	3,012	75,450
Employee Benefits	369	982	554	853	422	2,093	1,907	1,372	665	1,056	1,062	115	11,450
Direct Operating Exp.	488	384	1,121	878	1,481	2,757	1,589	1,988	404	1,635	340	361	13,476
Advertising & Promotion	941	945	739	692	1,121	1,486	2,356	1,128	1,175	856	994	941	13,374
Utilities	535	1,212	676	1,215	443	1,355	571	1,960	607	1,486	194	411	10,665
Administrative & General	69	828	533	166	291	530	419	406	600	210	172	223	4,447
Repairs & Maintenance	99	73	554	243	1,284	1,894	1,365	884	404	1,382	166	17	8,365
Occupancy Costs													0
Rent	1,200	1,200	1,200	1,200	1,200	1,200	1,200	1,200	1,200	1,200	1,200	1,200	14,400
Property Taxes	1,903	0	0	0	0	0	0	0	2,585	0	0	0	4,488
Other Taxes	0	0	0	0	0	0	0	0	0	0	0	0	0
Property Insurance	1,457	0	0	1,456	0	0	1,675	0	0	1,628	0	0	6,216
Interest	0	0	0	0	0	0	0	0	0	0	0	0	0
Other Deductions	0	0	0	0	0	0	0	0	0	0	0	900	900
Total Cash Disbursements:	16,321	14,807	16,180	18,822	24,353	36,058	50,890	41,209	27,059	21,197	13,285	10,824	291,005

Section Two: Financial Data

	1	2	3	4	5	6	7	8	9	10	11	12	Total
Cash Flow From Operations													
Cash Receipts	10,517	10,882	15,186	18,177	32,203	45,460	58,890	55,986	28,705	19,343	9,908	5,229	310,486
Less: Cash Disbursements	16,321	14,807	16,180	18,822	24,353	36,058	50,890	41,209	27,059	21,197	13,285	10,824	291,005
Net From Operations	(5,804)	(3,925)	(994)	(645)	7,850	9,402	8,000	14,777	1,646	(1,854)	(3,377)	(5,595)	19,481
Cash on Hand													
Opening Balance	0	(5,804)	(9,729)	(10,723)	(11,368)	(3,518)	5,884	13,884	28,661	30,307	28,453	25,076	
Plus: New Loan (Debt)													
Plus: New Investment													
Plus: Sale of Fixed Assets													
Plus: Net From Operations	(5,804)	(3,925)	(994)	(645)	7,850	9,402	8,000	14,777	1,646	(1,854)	(3,377)	(5,595)	19,481
Total Cash Available	(5,804)	(9,729)	(10,723)	(11,368)	(3,518)	5,884	13,884	28,661	30,307	28,453	25,076	19,481	
Less: Debt Reduction													
Less: New Fixed Assets													
Less: Dividends to Stockholders													
Less: Stock Redemption													
Less: Loans to Officers													
Total Cash Paid Out	0	0	0	0	0	0	0	0	0	0	0	0	
Cash Position—Ending Balance	(5,804)	(9,729)	(10,723)	(11,368)	(3,518)	5,884	13,884	28,661	30,307	28,453	25,076	19,481	

Stefanie's Restaurant
Cash Flow Projections—By Quarter, Year Two

	1st Quarter	2nd Quarter	3rd Quarter	4th Quarter	Total
Cash Receipts					
Food Sales	29,171	81,375	125,490	30,112	266,148
Beverage Sales	11,073	24,048	31,351	7,752	74,224
Sales Receivables	0	0	0	0	0
Other Income	300	300	300	300	1,200
Total Cash Receipts	**40,544**	**105,723**	**157,141**	**38,164**	**341,572**
Cash Disbursements					
Cost of Sales, Food	12,386	34,552	53,283	12,786	113,007
Cost of Sales, Beverages	4,109	8,924	11,635	2,877	27,545
Controllable Expenses					
Payroll	11,244	19,224	40,918	11,629	83,015
Employee Benefits	2,096	3,705	4,338	2,456	12,595
Direct Operating Exp.	2,192	5,628	4,379	2,625	14,824
Advertising & Promotion	2,888	3,629	5,125	3,070	14,712
Utilities	2,665	3,314	3,452	2,300	11,731
Administrative & General	1,573	1,086	1,568	666	4,893
Repairs & Maintenance	799	3,763	2,918	1,722	9,202
Occupancy Costs					
Rent	3,600	3,600	3,600	3,600	14,400
Property Taxes	2,093	0	0	2,844	4,937
Other Taxes	0	0	0	0	0
Property Insurance	1,709	1,709	1,709	1,709	6,836
Interest	0	0	1,500	900	2,400
Other Deductions	0	0	0	0	0
Total Cash Disbursements:	**47,354**	**89,134**	**134,425**	**49,184**	**320,097**
Cash Flow From Operations					
Cash Receipts	40,544	105,723	157,141	38,164	341,572
Less: Cash Disbursements	47,354	89,134	134,425	49,184	320,097
Net From Operations	**(6,810)**	**16,589**	**22,716**	**(11,020)**	**21,475**
Cash on Hand					
Opening Balance	0	(6,810)	9,779	12,495	
Plus: New Loan (Debt)	20,000				
Plus: New Investment	10,000				
Plus: Sale of Fixed Assets					
Plus: Net From Operations	(6,810)	16,589	22,716	(11,020)	
Total Cash Available	23,190	9,779	32,495	1,475	
Less: Debt Reduction			20,000		
Less: New Fixed Assets	30,000				
Less: Dividends to Stockholders					
Less: Stock Redemption					
Less: Loans to Officers					
Total Cash Paid Out	**30,000**	**0**	**20,000**	**0**	
Cash Position —Ending Balance	**(6,810)**	**9,779**	**12,495**	**1,475**	**1,475**

Section Two: Financial Data

Stefanie's Restaurant
Cash Flow Projections—By Quarter, Year Three

	1st Quarter	2nd Quarter	3rd Quarter	4th Quarter	Total
Cash Receipts					
Food Sales	32,088	89,512	138,039	33,123	292,762
Beverage Sales	12,180	26,452	34,486	8,528	81,646
Sales Receivables	0	0	0	0	0
Other Income	300	300	300	300	1,200
Total Cash Receipts	44,568	116,264	172,825	41,951	375,608
Cash Disbursements					
Cost of Sales, Food	12,193	34,015	52,455	12,587	111,250
Cost of Sales, Beverages	3,898	8,465	11,036	2,729	26,128
Controllable Expenses					
Payroll	12,347	21,146	45,010	12,792	91,295
Employee Benefits	2,305	4,075	4,772	2,702	13,854
Direct Operating Exp.	2,412	6,190	4,817	2,887	16,306
Advertising & Promotion	3,176	3,992	5,637	3,377	16,182
Utilities	2,932	3,646	3,797	2,530	12,905
Administrative & General	1,730	1,194	1,724	732	5,380
Repairs & Maintenance	878	4,139	3,210	1,894	10,121
Occupancy Costs					
Rent	3,600	3,600	3,600	3,600	14,400
Property Taxes	2,302	0	0	3,128	5,430
Other Taxes	0	0	0	0	0
Property Insurance	1,880	1,880	1,880	1,880	7,520
Interest	0	0	0	900	900
Other Deductions	0	0	0	0	0
Total Cash Disbursements:	49,653	92,342	137,938	51,738	331,671
Cash Flow From Operations					
Cash Receipts	44,568	116,264	172,825	41,951	375,608
Less: Cash Disbursements	49,653	92,342	137,938	51,738	331,671
Net From Operations	(5,085)	23,922	34,887	(9,787)	43,937
Cash on Hand					
Opening Balance	0	(5,085)	18,837	53,724	
Plus: New Loan (Debt)					
Plus: New Investment					
Plus: Sale of Fixed Assets					
Plus: Net From Operations	(5,085)	23,922	34,887	(9,787)	
Total Cash Available	(5,085)	18,837	53,724	43,937	
Less: Debt Reduction					
Less: New Fixed Assets					
Less: Dividends to Stockholders					
Less: Stock Redemption					
Less: Loans to Officers					
Total Cash Paid Out	0	0	0	0	
Cash Position - Ending Balance	(5,085)	18,837	53,724	43,937	43,937

results—there should be enough cash to pay back the loan principal of $20,000 as well as the interest on the loan ($20,000 @10% interest for 9 months = $1,500) during the third quarter. Although repayment of the loan won't provide Stefanie's Restaurant with much cash flow during the second year, it will eliminate the debt for the expansion project and set up the business for stronger cash flows in the future.

Finally, the projected cash flows for year two reveal that there will be negative cash flows from operation during the first quarter. Stefanie Clark must, once again, take this into account in her planning and arrange to either loan the business the necessary cash or arrange a short-term operating loan from another source to get the business through the cycle.

Explanation of Year Three Cash Flow Projections

The third year cash flow projections show that Stefanie's Restaurant and its owner are finally going to see some rewards after working for minimal salary.

The reduction of the food cost and beverage cost to more acceptable levels has had a tremendous impact on the cash flow from operations.

The decision Stefanie Clark now has to make is whether or not to pay down some of the initial debt that was incurred when the restaurant was started, use the cash to expand even further, or draw the cash out of the business in the form of a dividend. If the projections prove to be accurate—and they should since the estimates were conservative for reducing food and beverage costs during the first two years and were high for increasing operating expenses—Stefanie Clark has a nice problem to face.

You should notice that only the most important cash flow items are annotated. Such annotation helps you remember your thinking at some later time—and helps avoid repeating errors. It also makes your projections much more believable, since the numbers will be seen to have more foundation than guesswork.

Application of Funds Statement

This is a handy addition to your cash flow analysis. Your banker may be interested in a source and applications statement, which is a slightly more formal version that your CPA could help you with, but this is handy when you are looking at ways of financing major acquisitions.

Application of Funds Statement
for Stefanie's Restaurant

Use of Funds	Total Amount Required:	From Equity:	From Loans:	From Others:
Leasehold Improvements				
Dining Deck	$12,000		$12,000	
Rest Rooms	10,000	$2,000	8,000	
Furniture, Fixtures & Equip.	6,500	6,500		
Inventories	1,500	1,500		
Cash Reserves	5,000		5,000	
Totals	$35,000	$10,000	$25,000	

• • •

The next section, Deviation Analysis, takes a more formal approach to using a budget. It uses the cash flow and income statements to set up a red-flag system. If over a three- or six-month time period your projections are seriously off, take the time to understand why the deviations have happened before changing your projections and your business operations. Then make the changes based on informed knowledge rather than hunch, a major reason to document your assumptions in your financial statements.

G. Deviation Analysis

For most restaurants, the cash flow projection for one year provides an adequate operating budget. You may want to break down some of the cash flow items more finely to ensure greater control, but in any case the cash flow projection is the basis for your budgets.

While anyone can learn to stay within a budget, only the best managers can draw up budgets worth staying within. While a well-thought-out cash flow projection doesn't guarantee a good budget, you can be sure that a budget drawn up without such projections won't be worth following.

Budget deviation analysis (BDA) is a direct control on your operation. It will help you hold down costs and increase profits at a time cost of about one evening per month. It is an essential tool and should not be ignored even if everything is going well.

BDA must be performed periodically, at least monthly, if it is to be effective. BDA provides one of the best sources of current information available to you. Use it. Done properly, it will tell you at a glance which parts of your restaurant are out of control and which ones are exceeding expectations.

The next pages are BDA forms, which you should modify to suit the particular needs of your restaurant. Columns C and D are derived from actual and budgeted figures. Experience will tell you which deviations—and of what magnitude—are significant. Any deviation, positive or negative, should be carefully examined and the reasons for its existence understood. Next, corrective action should be taken (if the deviation is working against you), or the serendipitous improvement in performance should be exploited (if the deviation is in your favor).

For example, suppose that utilities, budgeted for $200 in January, actually cost $340. Why? The weather was exceptionally cold, insulation was installed toward the end of the month, and a broken skylight was replaced on February 1. The indicated action was to cut utilities expense as soon as possible (which was done). If close attention had not been paid to the utility bill, that cost could easily have gotten out of hand. Again, suppose sales were $18,000 in January, not the anticipated (budgeted) $14,600. What went right? Careful attention to a positive deviation can pay off in greatly increased profits.

Year-to-date BDA is another good financial tool. If more expenditures fall in one month than were expected, you will find a corresponding lowering of expenditures the preceding or following month. The year-to-date BDA helps to level out these swings. Used with the monthly BDAs, this form will save you some unnecessary arithmetic and worry,

Budget deviation analysis will help you hold down costs and increase profits.

Budget Deviation Analysis by Month
From the Income Statement
For the Month of _____

	A Actual for Month	B Budget for Month	C Deviation (B-A)	D % Deviation (C/B x 100)
Sales				
Food				
Beverage				
Total Sales				
Cost of Sales				
Food				
Beverage				
Total Cost of Sales				
Gross Profit				
Other Income				
Total Income				
Controllable Expenses				
Payroll				
Employee Benefits				
Direct Operating Exp.				
Advertising & Promotion				
Utilities				
Administrative & General				
Repairs & Maintenance				
Total Controllable Exp.				
Income Before Occupancy Costs				
Occupancy Costs				
Rent				
Property Taxes				
Other Taxes				
Property Insurance				
Total Occupancy Costs				
Income Before Interest and Dep.				
Interest				
Depreciation				
Restaurant Profit				
Other Deductions				
Income Before Income Taxes				

Budget Deviation Analysis Year-to-Date
From the Income Statement
Year-to-Date_____

	A Actual Year-to-Date	B Budget Year-to-Date	C Deviation (B-A)	D % Deviation (C/B x 100)
Sales				
Food				
Beverage				
Total Sales				
Cost of Sales				
Food				
Beverage				
Total Cost of Sales				
Gross Profit				
Other Income				
Total Income				
Controllable Expenses				
Payroll				
Employee Benefits				
Direct Operating Exp.				
Advertising & Promotion				
Utilities				
Administrative & General				
Repairs & Maintenance				
Total Controllable Exp.				
Income Before Occupancy Costs				
Occupancy Costs				
Rent				
Property Taxes				
Other Taxes				
Property Insurance				
Total Occupancy Costs				
Income Before Interest and Dep.				
Interest				
Depreciation				
Restaurant Profit				
Other Deductions				
Income Before Income Taxes				

Calculations:
A. Add current month's actual to last month's year-to-date analysis.
B. Add current month's budget to last month's year-to-date analysis.

Section Two: Financial Data

**Budget Deviation Analysis by Month
From the Cash Flow
For the Month of _____**

	A Actual for Month	B Budget for Month	C Deviation (B-A)	D % Deviation (C/B x 100)
Cash Receipts				
Food Sales				
Beverage Sales				
Sales Receivables				
Other Income				
Total Cash Receipts				
Cash Disbursements				
Cost of Sales, Food				
Cost of Sales, Beverages				
Controllable Expenses				
Payroll				
Employee Benefits				
Direct Operating Exp.				
Advertising & Promotion				
Utilities				
Administrative & General				
Repairs & Maintenance				
Occupancy Costs				
Rent				
Property Taxes				
Other Taxes				
Property Insurance				
Interest				
Other Deductions				
Total Cash Disbursements:				
Cash Flow From Operations				
Cash Receipts				
Less: Cash Disbursements				
Net From Operations				
Cash on Hand				
Opening Balance				
Plus: New Loan (Debt)				
Plus: New Investment				
Plus: Sale of Fixed Assets				
Plus: Net From Operations				
Total Cash Available				
Less: Debt Reduction				
Less: New Fixed Assets				
Less: Dividends to Stockholders				
Less: Stock Redemption				
Less: Loans to Officers				
Total Cash Paid Out				
Cash Position—Ending Balance				

Budget Deviation Analysis Year-to-Date
From the Cash Flow, Year-to-Date _____

	A Actual Year-to-Date	B Budget Year-to-Date	C Deviation (B-A)	D % Deviation (C/B x 100)
Cash Receipts				
Food Sales				
Beverage Sales				
Sales Receivables				
Other Income				
Total Cash Receipts				
Cash Disbursements				
Cost of Sales, Food				
Cost of Sales, Beverages				
Controllable Expenses				
Payroll				
Employee Benefits				
Direct Operating Exp.				
Advertising & Promotion				
Utilities				
Administrative & General				
Repairs & Maintenance				
Occupancy Costs				
Rent				
Property Taxes				
Other Taxes				
Property Insurance				
Interest				
Other Deductions				
Total Cash Disbursements:				
Cash Flow From Operations				
Cash Receipts				
Less: Cash Disbursements				
Net From Operations				
Cash on Hand				
Opening Balance				
Plus: New Loan (Debt)				
Plus: New Investment				
Plus: Sale of Fixed Assets				
Plus: Net From Operations				
Total Cash Available				
Less: Debt Reduction				
Less: New Fixed Assets				
Less: Dividends to Stockholders				
Less: Stock Redemption				
Less: Loans to Officers				
Total Cash Paid Out				
Cash Position - Ending Balance				

Calculations:
A. Add current month's actual to last month's year-to-date analysis.
B. Add current month's budget to last month's year-to-date analysis.

Section Two: Financial Data 97

as well as check the accuracy and effectiveness of your projections. With experience, your budgeting will become more exact, affording you greater control over your business and profits.

As with the other control documents, you should adapt the suggested formats that follow to fit your particular needs. Your accountant should be helpful here, but you have to be the person who decides what information should be reflected by BDA.

Another reason for adopting the Uniform System of Accounts for Restaurants is that you can then do a BDA comparing both your budgeted and actual figures with national (or regional or local) averages. Budget Deviation Analysis forms are included to compare with National Restaurant Association statistics. The NRA statistics included here are for full-menu table service restaurants located outside of metropolitan statistical areas (the most appropriate comparison for Stefanie's Restaurant), but a variety of other statistics are provided as well by the National Restaurant Association. Use the statistical base that most closely resembles your restaurant operation.

You will also notice that "Column D: % Deviation" will magnify small numbers. If Administrative and General is budgeted at $50/month and comes in at $100, the percentage deviation is 100 percent. This is deliberate. Large dollar deviations show up clearly in "Column C: Deviation," but small deviations can collectively become fairly large, and have a devastating cumulative effect on profits. This is another area where a bit of computer power takes the drudgery (and opportunities for error) out of repetitive monthly calculations. Set your tolerances. Then follow up on all significant deviations.

A Sample Budget Deviation Analysis

A budget deviation analysis has been prepared for Stefanie's Restaurant and follows on page 98. The budget deviation analysis has been prepared by comparing the actual year one income statement percentages for Stefanie's Restaurant with the median averages from the National Restaurant Association's *Restaurant Industry Operations Report, 1991*. The analysis could also have been done by comparing with industry averages on a per seat basis, by comparing with the projected or budgeted first year figures, or by comparing with previous years' figures if they had been available. Since this was the first year of operation, Stefanie's Restaurant wanted to compare actual results with national averages.

The analysis reveals that Stefanie's Restaurant has a higher percentage of beverage sales than the national average and a corresponding lower percentage of food sales. This may be due to the fact that a number of boaters visit Stefanie's Restaurant for cocktails and snacks; it may be due to the fact that there are several wineries in the area and people visiting them tend to buy the wines when they eat at the restaurant; it

Budget Deviation Analysis for Year One
Comparison of Income Statement Percentages
Stefanie's Restaurant Actual with
National Restaurant Association Statistics

	A NRA* Median Statistics %	B Stefanie's Restaurant Actual %	C Deviation % Points (B-A)	D % Deviation (C/B x 100)
Sales				
Food	88.5	78.2	-10.3	-13.2%
Beverage	17.8	21.8	4.0	18.3%
Total Sales	100.0	100.0	0.0	0.0%
Cost of Sales				
Food	36.9	42.5	5.6	13.2%
Beverage	29.1	37.1	8.0	21.6%
Total Cost of Sales	35.2	41.3	6.1	14.8%
Gross Profit	64.9	58.7	-6.2	-10.6%
Other Income	0.6	0.3	-0.3	-100.0%
Total Income	65.9	59.0	-6.9	-11.7%
Controllable Expenses				
Payroll	30.1	24.4	-5.7	-23.4%
Employee Benefits	4.4	3.7	-0.7	-18.9%
Direct Operating Exp.	5.4	4.4	-1.0	-22.7%
Advertising & Promotion	1.5	4.3	2.8	65.1%
Utilities	3.2	3.4	0.2	5.9%
Administrative & General	3.4	1.4	-2.0	-142.9%
Repairs & Maintenance	1.9	2.7	0.8	29.6%
Total Controllable Exp.	50.5	44.3	-6.2	-14.0%
Income Before Occupancy Costs	12.6	14.7	2.1	14.3%
Occupancy Costs				
Rent	4.3	4.7	0.4	8.5%
Property Taxes	0.8	1.5	0.7	46.7%
Other Taxes	1.1	0.0	-1.1	ERR
Property Insurance	1.2	2.0	0.8	40.0%
Total Occupancy Costs	6.4	8.1	1.7	21.0%
Income Before Interest and Dep.	6.8	6.6	-0.2	-3.0%
Interest	1.3	0.3	-1.0	-333.3%
Depreciation	2.6	1.5	-1.1	-73.3%
Restaurant Profit	4.0	4.8	0.8	16.7%
Other Deductions	1.3	0.0	-1.3	ERR
Income Before Income Taxes	3.8	4.8	1.0	20.8%

*Exhibit A-23, Full-Menu Table Service Statement of Income and Expenses—Ratio to Total Sales, Non-Metropolitian Location, page 43, Restaurant Industry Operations Report, National Restaurant Association, 1991.

may be due to the fact that Stefanie's Restaurant sells a lot of sandwiches and other lower priced items and, therefore, the percentage for beverages is higher (a $2.00 beer with a $5.00 hamburger results in beverage sales of 28.6 percent while the same $2.00 beer with a $14.00 steak results in beverage sales of 12.5 percent); or—more likely than not—it is probably due to some combination of these reasons.

Stefanie's Restaurant should be more concerned with the fact that its food cost and beverage cost are both higher than national averages and both higher than what was projected when the menu pricing was done. An analysis of these costs on a month-to-month basis shows that the percentages are much higher in the beginning of the year when the restaurant was just getting started and also during the slower periods of the year when there tends to be more waste and it is more difficult to utilize leftovers. Whatever the reason, the deviation analysis indicates that there should be some cause for concern. The reasons need to be identified and corrected. The higher food cost and beverage cost result in a lower gross profit when compared to the national averages.

Stefanie's Restaurant has a much lower labor cost percentage than the NRA averages. While this may be viewed as good, care should be taken to ensure that service is not suffering because of the lower labor cost. The most likely explanation for the lower cost is because the owner, Stefanie Clark, is working many hours for a very low wage. Stefanie realized that she would not make a lot of money the first few years and hoped that her rewards would come in later years through the increase in her equity and by increased cash flow since the restaurant is not burdened with a great deal of debt. The fact that the expense for employee benefits is low is explained because Stefanie's Restaurant utilizes mostly part-time, seasonal and temporary employees because of the cyclical nature of the business. Therefore, the only employee benefits offered are those required by law.

The high rate of advertising and promotion is primarily the result of a heavy marketing campaign since the restaurant is new and needed heavy promotion during the first year.

Overall, Stefanie's Restaurant has lower controllable expenses than the national average—primarily due to the lower labor costs—and, as a result, a greater income before occupancy costs.

Total occupancy costs for Stefanie's Restaurant are higher than national averages due primarily to the cost of rent and the cost of property insurance. Both of these are high because of the restaurant's location on the water.

Finally, the interest and depreciation expenses are lower and can be attributed to the fact that Stefanie's Restaurant leases, rather than owns, the building. If the building were owned, interest on the mortgage and depreciation on the building would be included here.

Overall, Stefanie's Restaurant should be pleased with its operating results for the first year. The restaurant profit is above national averages and the restaurant is profitable (both in terms of profits and in terms of cash flow). Stefanie Clark should be pleased with her first year's efforts.

One note of caution, however, industry averages are only that, averages, and should be used as guidelines for comparison and not as absolute values to be measured against. They are only one tool—albeit a valuable one—to be used for analyzing a restaurant. Percentages are also greatly affected by total sales (e.g., if total sales doubled, the cost of insurance would remain the same but the cost as a percentage of sales would be reduced from 2.0 percent to 1.0 percent). Comparisons with previous operating data, with budgets, and with projections should also be done. Each provides a somewhat different picture. The trick is to make an overall assessment and decide on a plan of action after looking at information from a variety of sources.

H. Historical Financial Reports

A record of what happened in the past is an integral part of your business plan. For most business deals, balance sheets and income statements for the past three years are sufficient.

The third major component of your past financial records is tax statements. Since they must be filed at least annually, they provide a summary of what you earned, how you earned it, and what your deductible expenses were. If you decide to sell your business, these tax statements will be the most important substantiation of your asking price, and will surely be requested and examined by prospective purchasers.

If you don't yet have an accountant, go directly to the nearest IRS office well in advance of payment day and go over your business records with one of their representatives. By doing so, you gain the benefit of free advice from experts and get an insight into the best ways to handle your business taxes. The IRS will even help you set up your record keeping system to minimize the problems of preparing tax returns.

The IRS is more concerned with helping businesses properly handle their financial responsibilities (taxes) than you may have thought. It makes their job easier. They provide a number of free tax seminars for small businesses, which can be useful, especially if you are trying to handle your own taxes.

Tax records can be used as an additional source of information. For example, copies of wage and deduction statements help in making projections. Payroll records can help settle unemployment claims; they have a certain legal weight, especially in situations where it's your word against that of a disgruntled former employee.

Most business owners know that it pays to hire a competent accountant to handle taxes. The tax code has something like 40,000 pages, changes frequently, and contains so many booby traps (for businesses as well as individuals) that it just doesn't make sense to try to do your returns yourself. Your job is making your restaurant profitable. Your accountant's job is making sure that you don't pay more taxes than you are legally required to pay. And you can't do both jobs.

If you do not have clear, accurate and well-substantiated historical financial records, or if you have lied to minimize your tax liabilities, you have only cheated yourself. In the first case, you've only demonstrated your incompetence. In the second case, you've simply lowered the performance level of the business, thus making it a worse risk for a lender. Either way, it just isn't worth it.

A record of what happened in the past is an integral part of your business plan.

I. Summary

Budgeting, balancing objectives with reality, then guiding your restaurant to achieve your goals within the budget constraints, is a hard test of managerial ability.

With the exception of the historical financial reports, which reflect past management decisions, the Financial Data section stresses the importance of making and documenting careful assumptions about the objectives of your restaurant as the first step in preparing financial projections.

Your income and cash flow projections are the basis of your planning efforts. They help set up a series of objectives: At what level do you hit break-even? What are the budget items to monitor closely—monthly or more often? What profit levels do you want to achieve, and what sales levels are needed to reach those profit goals?

Planning is the key to business success.

Deviation analysis puts the controls more directly to work by providing an early warning system pinpointing trouble before it gets out of hand. By measuring progress toward the goals set in your income and cash flow projections, and clamping down on costs with deviation analysis, your management workload will be greatly reduced.

The financial statements are not intended to be straitjackets. They should instead free you from the most pressing problem most small-business owners/managers face: How do you find time for managing when there are so many brush fires to be put out? Your single most important asset is your time. To make effective use of your time, early planning is a necessity, *not* a luxury.

The financial statements are the easiest part of the business plan. The hard part, the thinking that goes into establishing the goals and strategies of your business and the effort that goes into staffing and managing people, has to be done before your financial projections can make sense. Your financial projections are a model of your restaurant, based on your assumptions and experience and perceptions of your markets.

This model can provide the most effective control over your restaurant—or it can degenerate into a "fun with numbers" game. The choice is yours. You must take the time to think through your assumptions and objectives. You must make your assumptions as clear and as well defined as you can. And you must be prepared to continually review and reevaluate those assumptions and objectives.

Set aside time to review the information your financial statements provide. An excellent practice followed by many managers is to set aside an afternoon or evening each week, away from the telephone and other interruptions, for planning and review. If you feel you cannot afford the time, you have the clearest indication that you must plan, that you must take the time now.

Remember: Planning is the key to business success.

Section Three: The Financing Proposal

The purpose of this section is to help you turn your business plan into a financing proposal that fits your business needs and capital constraints.

The financing proposal is slanted toward a banker's needs. In very few situations, other capital sources should be approached—venture capital firms or investment bankers, for example. If your deal is large enough and the anticipated payoff is sufficiently high (financing needs of over $1 million, with an anticipated payout rate greater than 40 percent annually are two rough measures), your banker and other advisors will steer you to the right people. Otherwise, don't waste your time or theirs. Most deals never get beyond the first screening (five percent or so make it through) and only a handful of those get venture capital or go public. If your deal is attractive enough to warrant attention, you will want to tailor your proposal to the needs of your intended audience, a process well beyond the scope of this handbook and one that requires detailed knowledge of the players involved.

For the rest of us with more modest deals, turn to your banker first. Your banker may refer you to a local venture capital club or other source of equity, but start with your banker. If you need more equity than you have available, check with your accountant and lawyer, who may be in touch with individuals who invest in local or start-up deals. If you don't have a banker and an accountant, you surely will have no need for specialized financing.

The business plan that you have developed throughout the preceding pages needs little alteration to become a first-rate financing proposal. Some areas of the plan will be of little use to your banker (personal histories can be replaced by resumes; deviation analysis won't be needed). The difference between a business plan and a financing proposal is one of emphasis rather than design. The main function of your plan is to enable you to understand and master the complexities of your business, whereas the function of the financing proposal is to show your prospective backers that you not only know what you are doing but will also make their investment as risk-free as possible.

Most bankers deal with small-business owners who don't understand the differences between types of financing, the importance of those distinctions to a business, and the banker's point of view. By showing some familiarity with how a business financing package looks from the banker's viewpoint, you will be on guard against two severe problems:

1. The banker who can't say "no" but who can't or won't provide adequate financing; and/or
2. The banker who gives the wrong loan for the wrong reasons.

You will also better understand the role of a bank in the financing process. Banks are not venture capitalists, not risk takers, not gamblers. They shouldn't be. Their business is investing other people's money, and they have to be cautious.

Restaurants are viewed by many bankers as notoriously bad investments.

Restaurants are viewed by many bankers as notoriously bad investments and many banks refuse to finance restaurants for a variety of reasons: low barriers to entry, little collateral value in used restaurant equipment, and hours required on site by the owner, just to name a few. Therefore, it is important that you prepare your financing proposal so that it clearly states what you need, the form that you need the financing in, and how and when you expect to repay the money. In addition, you should design the proposal to appeal to sources other than traditional lending institutions.

In the case of Stefanie's Restaurant, the initial funding was provided by Stefanie Clark from her savings and a loan from her parents. In addition, she kept the start-up costs low by renting space and purchasing used restaurant equipment where possible. Finally, she was willing to commit a great deal of time to make the restaurant a success, and she took a minimum salary. Based upon her first year's success and her commitment to the business, she now has an excellent chance of obtaining financing for the expansion from a bank.

Debt vs. Equity
When you go to your bank for a loan, you are seeking debt money, which you will repay over a period of time at an additional cost (interest). The money you invest in your business is ordinarily equity, that is, money that will not be repaid to you unless you sell a portion of your ownership. Debt financing doesn't lead to sharing ownership of your business with the financier. Equity financing does.

Control is another matter. Your banker may exert substantial control over your business through a legal loan document or through suggestions, but he or she doesn't own your business. Debt pays interest, usually for a finite time. Equity pays profits forever.

The distinction between debt and equity is important to your banker because the more debt there is in relation to equity, the higher the risk. A high debt-to-worth ratio (worth being roughly equivalent to equity, but may include some kinds of subordinated debt) indicates high risk and high risk costs high interest if you can find new debt money at all. Why? Because debt money is rented money, and the rent must be paid no matter how the business is doing. If you can't meet your debt payments, you go out of business.

Not only that, but a highly leveraged business (higher than normal debt-to-worth ratio for that kind of business) must earn more money. Sometimes it's possible to find so much debt money that the business never can get ahead. Without capital (permanent non-repayable money invested in the business), you can spin your wheels forever, a problem called overtrading. Sales-to-worth ratios are guidelines for this, and can help you pinpoint your capital needs relative to projected sales.

From a banker's viewpoint, the higher the debt, the riskier the deal. The longer the term, the riskier the deal. Short-term loans are less hazardous than long-term (with some exceptions) because if the loan goes sour, it does so in a hurry and can be easily detected, while a long-term decline can be almost imperceptible. The underlying issue—performance in the near future—can be predicted with much greater certainty than longer times allow.

The "Three C's of Credit": Character, Capacity and Capital.

Risk—the odds against an expected happening in the future—is just one of the elements in a credit decision.

Most bankers have been trained in the "Three C's of Credit": Character, Capacity, and Capital. Character reflects the willingness to pay (a record of nonpayment or a prior personal bankruptcy, for example, might cause a banker to view a person's character as too risky). Capacity and capital reflect ability to carry out the intent to pay. Experience is a factor here: Your experience in a given business affects your banker's perception of your ability to successfully run this business. Capital is obvious: A well-capitalized business is inherently less risky than an under-capitalized business. Costs will be lower, for example, and a capital cushion makes for sounder decisions.

Two other C's are often cited: Condition (of the economy and of the business) and Collateral. If the economy in your area is rolling off a cliff, the risk of your deal will be magnified. Collateral is useful as a means of tying you to the deal. Experience has shown that people who have their own assets on the line fight harder to make a deal work than people who are working with little of their own money at risk—and collateral also serves as a comfort factor for the banker. Bankers have no desire to be secondhand equipment dealers, or to sell off your stocks and bonds. But they like to have some recourse just in case your restaurant fails.

That's as it should be. Bankers are not in business to take risks or shoot for a long shot. (Nor should you be. Most studies of successful business owners show a profile of moderate risk taking. Not too conservative, but certainly not too eager to run unjustified risks.)

Another way that bankers and other financiers look at a deal is to consider the personal, financial, and economic factors that are involved. The personal factors include many intangibles (integrity, for example; try to define it) but your personal track record provides a clue. This is why a full resume has to be part of your financing proposal. If your banker has known you forever, fine—put it in anyway. Other bankers may not know you as well. Your education, experience, and history are important. The saying that "there are no small-business loans; just loans to small-business owners" is true. You'll probably have to sign personally for a loan while your business is small.

Financial factors have been covered in some detail in your financial statements, and if they are based on clearly spelled out, rational assumptions (which they will be if you have followed *The Restaurant Planning Guide* to this point), they will provide additional evidence of your personal commitment as well. Financial factors include product/service, marketing, competition, personnel and management elements, so all the work of Section One: The Business comes into play once more.

Economic factors may be beyond your control, but once again, will affect your banker's decision. Your restaurant idea might be poor today but wonderful tomorrow, and no banker would do you a favor by launching you into business at the wrong time. If times are tight, think carefully about a new venture (that doesn't mean not to pursue it, just to think it through especially carefully).

The key here: fit the financing to the need.

Assuming that you pass these rough sorting criteria, what comes next? Your business plan, tailored to the banker as a financing proposal, gains added credibility if you ask for the appropriate financing to fit your needs. You can research this ahead of time by involving your banker in your planning (never a bad idea anyway) and by asking your accountant.

The key here: fit the financing to the need.

When you projected your cash flow, you did two things that help determine the right financing mix for your restaurant. The deepest negative cash flows, both in net cash flow and cumulative cash flow, indicate how much money you need and when you need it. Projected cash receipts give you an inkling of how you will generate money to repay the loan or make good the investment. If you don't arrange for enough financing (of whatever kind), your deal will be dead. If you borrow more than you can service, your deal will also be dead. If you borrow at the wrong time, or for the wrong reasons, you aggravate the risks of being in business, risks that are already high.

Stefanie's Restaurant projected a worst negative cumulative cash flow in April of year one (see page 86). The solution: a term loan for operating funds. Protecting liquidity and ensuring adequate working capital are legitimate reasons to borrow—if you fit the financing to the need. The April year one shortfall is marked to show a need for the line of credit, another legitimate financing purpose, and one their banker looked on favorably.

Kinds of Bank Financing

Bankers customarily divide loans into three general categories:

1. Short-term financing is usually provided through notes to be paid within one year, usually in one sum. These notes are repaid through inventory turn or by converting receivables to cash within the time frame of the note.

2. Intermediate-term financing ranges from one to five years, and is usually repaid in fixed monthly payments or fixed principal payments plus interest. These loans are repaid from operating profits.

3. Long-term financing is provided for periods longer than five years. The most common example is real estate financing, where repayment is made on a prearranged schedule over a long period of years.

These loans may be secured or unsecured. A secured loan is backed by collateral—liens against your property, savings account or certificate of deposit, perhaps co-signed by someone with more assets—that would be applied to recover the loan in event of default.

An unsecured loan (sometimes called a signature or character loan) is one not backed by any collateral. These are almost always short-term loans, and are available only to the most credit worthy individuals and companies. The loan is backed up by your banker's faith in your character, capability and capital.

It helps to remember that bankers are in the business of investing money that isn't theirs, money that mustn't be subject to unusual risks. Banks do not and should not gamble with their depositors' money, and as a borrower you should understand this.

Your banker will lend your restaurant money if he or she feels comfortable with the risk. Bankers are under no obligation to lend money to a business that doesn't fit their risk tolerance—a frequent source of anger to credit seekers. Help your banker decide in your favor: lower the risk by keeping a low debt-to-worth ratio, make sure to have enough working capital to cover current liabilities, and match the financing request to your real needs. Note that from a banker's viewpoint, a loan should be repaid as soon as possible.

Long-term debt is for long-term needs, fixed assets, which will be used and paid for over the long haul. To pay this kind of debt off too fast is a mistake unless you are extremely well capitalized, in which case check with your banker and accountant first. They'll tell you.

Short-term debt is for short-term needs: seasonal inventory loans, short-run construction loans, short-term liquidity problems. These are repaid from the returns on specific transactions or series of transactions in a short period of time. If they are financed over a longer time span, the result is almost always deepening debt and the erosion of business assets. Even though your cash flow will look good by spreading the cost over a longer period, you would be violating a cardinal rule of borrowing: paying for a benefit after it has been exhausted. One reason bankers are hesitant to bail small businesses out of chronic trade debts is that those unpaid debts are evidence that the business is seriously mismanaged. Paying for a dead horse is bad business.

The line of credit (revolving or non-revolving) is a short-term tool that works like a credit card: you arrange before the need arises to have a certain amount of credit to draw against; then you pay it off (or renew it). The main thing to avoid is getting used to paying for last year's short-term needs with new debt—bad enough for an individual, but worse for a small business.

Friday night financing never works.

Intermediate-term debt is for those needs that last between one and five years. Most common are equipment loans and working capital loans for businesses undergoing rapid growth. By converting debt to earnings, and then retaining a portion of the earnings as capital, it is possible to grow using debt money. Don't plan on this, though, as it requires a farsighted banker, considerable risk, and profits high enough to handle the added interest costs.

For any kind of financing, a final word may be helpful: Friday night financing never works.

Always make sure your banker knows your needs well in advance. Then you won't get caught in a cash squeeze. Borrowing in a panic is outrageously dangerous. Don't do it.

Earlier in this section, we mentioned the problem of the banker who can't say no, yet won't provide the right amount of financing. If you have thought through your business plan, you will know how much you need, and when you'll need it. Make sure to get the right financing; less will only complicate matters. If your banker can give you good reasons to borrow less, pay attention—but think it through. Don't settle for enough money to get you into trouble but not enough to see you through.

Tell your banker what you need the money for, how it will be repaid—and why the deal makes good business sense. Your financing proposal does just that, and if based on your business plan and careful analysis, you should get the right financing.

A final reminder: Planning is the key to success.

Section Four: Supporting Documents

You will want to include any documents that lend support to statements you have made in the body of the business plan. Items included here will vary according to the needs and stage of development of your particular restaurant. The following list suggests some things that might be included:

1. Resumes: very important—see Functional Resumes, Appendix Two.
2. Credit information: forms included in Appendix Five.
3. Quotes or estimates.
4. Letters of intent from prospective customers.
5. Letters of support from credible people who know you.
6. Leases or buy/sell agreements.
7. Legal documents relevant to the business.
8. Census/demographic data.

A Sample Resume
Stefanie Clark

September 19__ to June 19__, Verbeyst University. Graduated with a BS degree in hotel management. During high school and college worked in a variety of local restaurants as a busgirl, waitress, hostess, and dining room supervisor.

June 19__ to September 19__, spent just over three years as assistant manager of Grandma Jo's House of Pasta at Grand Teeburg ski resort and summer camp in Wyoming.

September 19__ to September 19__, four years experience as assistant manager and unit manager at a variety of locations for Surf 'N Turf, a national restaurant chain.

A Sample Letter

Schnicklefritz Contractors, Inc.
9706 Congress Street
Halseyville, NY 14886
(607) 387-6093

September 14, 19__

Ms. Stefanie Clark
Stefanie's Restaurant
123 Main Street
Anytown, NY 14847

Dear Ms. Clark:

For the sum of $22,000, we propose to construct a dining deck measuring 42' x 42' and two rest rooms adjacent to the existing building occupied by Stefanie's Restaurant as shown on your outline sketch. Should you desire to undertake only part of the project, the cost of the deck would be $12,000 and the cost of the rest rooms would be $10,000.

These prices include the cost of all materials and the cost of all labor.

We would require a down payment of $6,000 and another $6,000 when the deck is completed, with the balance due upon completion of the entire project. If the above meets with your approval, please sign and return one copy of this letter.

Thank you,
Harry Schnicklefritz
President

Signed by:_____

Date:_____

A Sample Letter of Reference

John Burdick, III
234 Firehouse Drive
Horseheads, NY 12345

November 24, 19__

To Whom it May Concern:

It is a pleasure to write this letter of recommendation for Stefanie's Restaurant, Inc.

Last summer my daughter, Maura, was married on the dock at Stefanie's Restaurant and the reception for 120 people was held under a tent on the restaurant lawn. Ms. Stefanie Clark and the entire staff at the restaurant did an outstanding job with all aspects of the affair. The food was excellent, the staff personable and efficient, and the guests were pleased with all aspects of the arrangements.

I was extremely pleased with the way Stefanie's Restaurant met its commitment and would not hesitate to have an affair with them again.

Yours,

John Burdick, III

Floor Plan

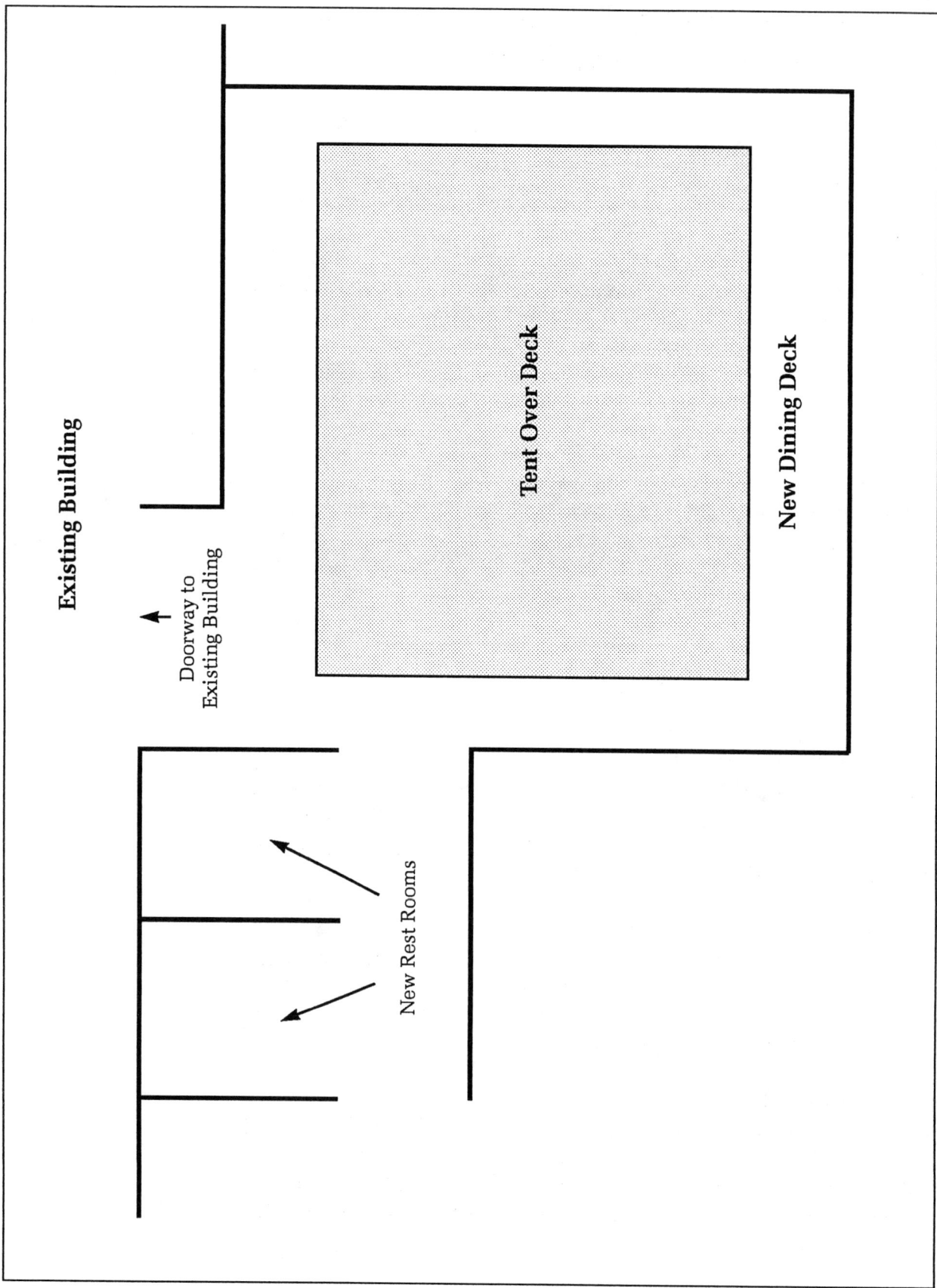

Appendix One:
A Sample Partnership Agreement and Corporate Checklist

These forms have been made available to Upstart Publishing Company, Inc., by General Business Services, Inc., of Rockville, MD. GBS is a nationwide company providing tax and business counseling services to small businesses.

We have modified the forms. To obtain originals, ask your local GBS representative for GBS form 89927: Partnership Agreement, or GBS form 89929: Corporate Checklist.

A Sample Partnership Agreement
Agreement made _____, 19___, between _____, City of _____, County of _____, State of _____, and _____ of _____ (address), City of _____, County of _____, State of _____, hereinafter referred to as partners.

Item One: Name, Purpose and Domicile
The name of the partnership shall be _____.
The partnership shall be conducted for the purposes of _____. The principal place of business shall be at _____ unless relocated by majority consent of the partners.

Item Two: Duration of Agreement
The term of this agreement shall be for _____ years, commencing on _____, 19__, and terminating on _____, 19 , unless sooner terminated by mutual consent of the parties or by operation of the provisions of this agreement.

Item Three: Contribution
Each partner shall contribute _____ dollars ($_____) on or before _____, 19__ to be used by the partnership to establish its capital position. Any additional contribution required of partners shall only be determined and established in accordance with Item Seventeen.

Item Four: Books and Records
Books of accounts shall be maintained by the partners, and proper entries made therein of all sales, purchases, receipts, payments, transactions, and property of the partnership, and the books of accounts and all records of the partnership shall be retained at the principal place of business as specified in Item One herein. Each partner shall have free access at all times to all books and records maintained relative to the partnership business.

Item Five: Division of Profits and Losses
Each partner shall be entitled to _____ percent (___%) of the net profits of the business and all losses occurring in the course of the business shall be borne in the same proportion, unless the losses are occasioned by the willful neglect or default, and not mere mistake or error, of any of the partners, in which case the loss so incurred shall be made good by the partner through whose neglect or default the losses shall arise. Distribution of profits shall be made on the _____ day of _____ each year.

Item Six: Performance
Each partner shall apply all of his experience, training, and ability in discharging his assigned functions in the partnership and in the performance of all work that may be necessary or advantageous to further business interests of the partnership.

Item Seven: Business Expenses
The rent of the buildings where the partnership business shall be carried on, and the cost of repairs and alterations, all rates, taxes, payments for insurance, and other expenses in respect to the buildings used by the partnership, and the wages for all persons employed by the partnership are all to become payable on the account of the partnership. All losses incurred shall be paid out of the capital of the partnership or the profits arising from the partnership business, or, if both shall be deficient, by the partners on a pro rata basis, in proportion to their original contribution.

Item Eight: Accounting
The fiscal year of the partnership shall be from _____ to _____ of each year. On the _____ day of _____, commencing in 19___, and on the _____ day of _____ in each succeeding year, a general accounting shall be made and taken by the partners of all sales, purchases, receipts, payments, and transactions of the partnership during the preceding fiscal year, and of all the capital property and current liabilities of the partnership. The general accounting shall be written in the partnership account books and signed in each book by each partner immediately after it is completed. After the signature of each partner is entered, each partner shall keep one of the books

and shall be bound by every account, except that if any manifest error is found therein by any partner and shown to the other partners within _____ months after the error shall have been noted by all of them, the error shall be rectified.

Item Nine: Separate Debts
No partner shall enter into any bond or become surety, security, bail or co-signer for any person, partnership or corporation, or knowingly condone anything whereby the partnership property may be attached or be taken in execution, without the written consent of the other partners.

Each partner shall punctually pay his separate debts and indemnify the other partners and the capital and property of the partnership against his separate debts and all expenses relating thereto.

Item Ten: Authority
No partner shall buy goods or articles into any contract exceeding the value _____ dollars ($_____) without the prior consent in writing of the other partners; or the other partners shall have the option to take the goods or accept the contract on account of the partnership or let the goods remain the sole property of the partner who shall have obligated himself or herself.

Item Eleven: Employee Management
No partner shall hire or dismiss any person in the employment of the partnership without the consent of the other partners, except in cases of gross misconduct by the employee.

Item Twelve: Salary
No partner shall receive any salary from the partnership, and the only compensation to be paid shall be as provided in Items Five and Fourteen herein.

Item Thirteen: Death of a Partner
In the event of the death of one partner, the legal representative of the deceased partner shall remain as a partner in the firm, except that the exercising of the right on the part of the representative of the deceased partner shall not continue for a period in excess of _____ months, even though under the terms hereof a greater period of time is provided before the termination of this agreement. The original rights of the partners herein shall accrue to their heirs, executors, or assigns.

Item Fourteen: Advance Draws
Each partner shall be at liberty to draw out of the business in anticipation of the expected profits any sums that may be mutually agreed on, and the sums are to be drawn only after there has been entered in the books of the partnership the terms of agreement, giving the date, the amount to be drawn by the respective partners, the time at which the

sums shall be drawn, and any other conditions or matters mutually agreed on. The signatures of each partner shall be affixed thereon. The total sum of the advance draw for each partner shall be deducted from the sum that partner is entitled to under the distribution of profits as provided for in Item Five of this agreement.

Item Fifteen: Retirement
In the event any partner shall desire to retire from the partnership, he shall give _____ months notice in writing to the other partners and the continuing partners shall pay to the retiring partner at the termination of the _____ months notice the value of the interest of the retiring partner in the partnership. The value shall be determined by a closing of the books and a rendition of the appropriate profit and loss, trial balance, and balance sheet statements. All disputes arising therefrom shall be determined as provided in Item Eighteen.

Item Sixteen: Rights of Continuing Partners
On the retirement of any partner, the continuing partners shall be at liberty, if they so desire, to retain all trade names designating the firm name used, and each of the partners shall sign and execute assignments, instruments, or papers that shall be reasonably required for effectuating an amicable retirement.

Item Seventeen: Additional Contributions
The partners shall not have to contribute any additional capital to the partnership to that required under Item Three herein, except as follows: (1) each partner shall be required to contribute a proportionate share in additional contributions if the fiscal year closes with an insufficiency in the capital account of profits of the partnership to meet current expenses, or (2) the capital account falls below _____ dollars ($_____) for a period of _____ months.

Item Eighteen: Arbitration
If any differences shall arise between or among partners as to their rights or liabilities under this agreement, or under any instrument made in furtherance of the partnership business, the difference shall be determined and the instrument shall be settled by _____, acting as arbitrator, and his or her decision shall be final as to the contents and interpretations of the instrument and as to the proper mode of carrying the provision into effect.

Item Nineteen: Release of Debts
No partner shall compound, release, or discharge any debt that shall be due or owing to the partnership, without receiving the full amount thereof, unless that partner obtains the prior written consent of the other partners to the discharge of the indebtedness.

Item Twenty: Additions, Alterations, or Modifications
Where it shall appear to the partners that this agreement, or any terms and conditions contained herein, are in any way ineffective or deficient, or not expressed as originally intended, and any alteration or addition shall be deemed necessary, the partners will enter into, execute, and perform all further deeds and instruments as their counsel shall advise. Any addition, alteration, or modification shall be in writing, and no oral agreement shall be effective.

In witness whereof, the parties have executed this agreement on _____ the day and year first above written.
Courtesy of General Business Forms, Inc.

Corporate Checklist

A. The formation of a corporation constitutes the formation of a separate legal entity under state law. It is essential that the services of a competent local attorney be obtained to help the client file the Articles of Incorporation and meet the terms of the state law.

B. Below is a sample election for the corporation to be treated as a Section 1244 small business corporation. This is included so that the client may have it available to discuss with his or her attorney.

C. Following is a list of steps that will be necessary for a new corporation. It should not be deemed to be all inclusive. It is not intended to be used as substitution to the client for a competent attorney.

1. Incorporators: Have a meeting of the incorporators and determine the following:
    a. The corporate name
    b. The classes and number of shares to authorize
    c. Business purpose for which the corporation is formed
    d. Initial capital needed
    e. The directors
    f. Location of business
    g. The corporate officers and their salaries
    h. Check on thin incorporation

2. Determine start-up date: If the corporation is to take over a going business, a start-up date should be set at some time in the future, so that all steps can be taken without unnecessary haste.

3. Research the corporate name: Check at once with the Secretary of State to see if the corporate name is available.

4. Notify the following:
    a. Insurance company—have policies changed. May also be necessary to increase coverage.
    b. Creditors—inform all creditors of former business.
    c. Customers—inform all customers of former business.
    d. State and local authorities—such as the state unemployment and disability department and county assessor.

5. Transfer assets and liabilities: If the corporation is to take over a going business, determine what assets and liabilities are to be turned

over to the corporation, and what shares or notes are to be issued in exchange. Determine whether it qualifies as a tax-free exchange under IRC Sec. 3.

6. Select banks: Select bank or banks and furnish resolution authorizing who is to sign checks and negotiate loans.

7. Obtain identification number: File application for an identification number, Federal Form SS-4.

8. File for worker's compensation coverage.

9. File for unemployment insurance coverage.

10. Obtain any special licenses: Check on transfer of new license such as health department, liquor authority, Federal Alcohol, Tobacco, and Firearms (ATF), local business, etc.

11. File final returns: If the new corporation is taking over a going business, file sales tax, FICA tax, unemployment tax, and worker's compensation final returns for the old business after the corporation takes over the operation of the new business.

12. Determine federal unemployment requirements: Determine if final Form 940, employer's annual federal unemployment tax return is to be filed on old business.

13. Sales tax: Obtain a new sales tax vendor's license on the first day of business. Do not use any tax stamps purchased by the former business and do not use the plate from the former business.

14. Tax elections:

    a. Election under Sub-Chapter S - Determine if the corporation is going to elect to be taxed as a partnership under Sub-Chapter S. If so, prepare and file Form 2553, Election by Small Business Corporation, within thirty days after the first day of fiscal year of date new corporation commences to "do business."

    b. Section 1244 stock - If the corporation is eligible, issue stock in accordance with a written plan included in the minutes.

    c. Year ending - Determine the date the corporation's year will end.

    d. Accounting - Determine the method of accounting the corporation will use.

Appendix Two: Functional Resumes

Functional resumes are designed to provide financing agencies with the information needed to make decisions on managerial competence and experience. Ordinary resumes (such as the SBA Personal Information Sheet) can and do provide information such as job titles, dates, and salaries, but they do not answer such questions as: Did you have hiring and firing authority? Could you redesign work flow? And so forth.

A functional resume is usually self-designed since most jobs are not standard. The objective of this section is to help you design a functional resume that displays your experience and competence. Treat the following as suggestions, not ironclad rules.

A Suggested Format

Resumo of YOUR NAME

1. Business address
1. Telephone number

2. Home address
2. Telephone number

Business Experience
3. Most recent job first (include military experience).

Education
4. Most recent grade or diploma completed first.

Special Abilities and Interests
5. Hobbies, clubs, civic activities, etc.

Personal Information
6. Age, marital status, number of children.

References
7. Names and addresses of references (preferably business people).

Items four and five make a functional resume different from an ordinary, fact-oriented resume. They should describe jobs, education, and interests in functional terms. For example:

Standard Resume:

June 19__ to September 19__: Assistant manager, Grandma Jo's House of Pasta, Grand Teeburg, Wyoming. Beginning salary $160/week. Final salary $205/week.

Notice how the "standard" form is composed of brief detail. Contrast this with:

Functional Resume:

June 19__ to September 19__: Assistant Manager, Grandma Jo's House of Pasta, Grand Teeburg, Wyoming. Responsible for hiring, training and directing operations for a high volume cafeteria at Grand Teeburg ski resort and summer camp in Grand Teeburg, Wyoming. Directed operation employing 25 people on the evening shift and on the manager's days off. Implemented a new purchasing system that lowered food costs by three percentage points. Designed a scheduling program that increased overall sales per employee (FTE) by six percent with a resulting savings of almost $9,000 per year. Left to assume a position with a national chain which offered both career advancement and increased salary.

A good resume will also give the reader an understanding of what you can do.

Two final points: First, a good resume (functional or otherwise) should have no sizable time gaps (more than a month). Longer gaps create a credibility problem. Second, a good resume will do more than inform the reader of what you have done. It will also give the reader an understanding of what you can do, and this understanding, based on demonstrated performance, can make the difference between a positive response to a financing proposal and a negative one.

Your objective in items four and five is to show what you have accomplished and what abilities you have demonstrated. Item five, "Special Abilities and Interests," can be used to cover non-job achievements, interests, and personal skills, which may or may not be directly relevant to your employment. For instance, this is where off-the-job managerial experience would be stressed (e.g., local politics, coaching, club leadership).

Appendix Three:
Resources for Restaurateurs

National Restaurant Association. *Uniform System of Accounts for Restaurants*, sixth revised edition, 1990. This revised edition covers an introduction to accounting statements, examples of these statements based on the uniform system of accounts, simplified record keeping, restaurant controls, and a chart of accounts.

National Restaurant Association and Deloitte & Touche. *Restaurant Industry Operations Report, 1991*. National Restaurant Association, 1991. This annual report summarizes financial and operating data provided by members of the National Restaurant Association. The report includes specific financial information on full-menu and limited-menu tableservice restaurants, operators with no table service (fast-food), and cafeterias. National Restaurant Association, 1200 17th St., N.W., Washington, DC 20036 (202) 331-5900.

Grace Shugart. *Food for Fifty*. Macmillan, 1989. Provides basic information, recipes, and guidelines for preparing food in quantity. Specifically, the book discusses: weights, measures, recipe adjustment, menu planning, and recipes for special meals. Photographs and drawings are included to illustrate preparation techniques.

Costas Katsigris. *Pouring for Profit: A Guide to Bar and Beverage Management*. Wiley, 1983. Details on how to manage a bar and beverage operation efficiently and profitably. Planning, equipping, staffing, purchasing, managing inventory, and marketing are all discussed along with approaches to drink design and selection. More than 150 drawings and photographs illustrate techniques and equipment.

Cornell Quarterly. *The Essentials of Good Table Service*. Cornell Hotel and Restaurant Administration Quarterly, Ithaca, New York, 1988. This pamphlet covers the essentials of American, French and Russian table service from personal grooming to the details of serving crêpes suzette at the tableside. Buffet and banquet service are also discussed along with special sections on napkin folding and decorative ice carving.

The Educational Foundation of the National Restaurant Association. *Applied Food Service Sanitation*, 4th edition. Wiley & Sons, 1991. Teaches principles and practices to help reduce foodborne diseases and improve quality. The four sections cover sanitation and health, the serving of sanitary food, sanitary and safe food environments, and managing a sanitary and safe food service. Full of pictures and illustrations.

Jack D. Ninemeier. *Management of Food and Beverage Operations,* 2nd edition. American Hotel and Motel Association, 1990. Presents practical ideas for both commerical and institutional food-service operations. Covers menu design, nutrition, marketing, equipment, computers, and overall food cost.

Paul J. McVety. *Fundamentals of Menu Planning.* Van Nostrand Reinhold, 1989. Provides basic information about foods, management, and financing for menu planning. Intended to assist food-service managers in developing new menus. The numerous tables, forms and sample menus help instruct the reader and aid the book's discussion of nutrition, costing, merchandising, menu analysis and equipment selection.

Regina S. Baraban. *Successful Restaurant Design.* Van Nostrand Reinhold, 1989. This guide fully discusses both kitchen and dining room designs. The designs discussed integrate functional with aesthetic concerns. Sections of the book address design analysis and psychology, the customer's and management's perspective, and specific problem solving. Features color and black-and-white photographs.

Resources for Small Businesses

There are many excellent texts available on small-business management, but most are more appropriate for businesses with more than 100 employees. Check out your local library, college bookstores and these sources of small-business management information:

Upstart Publishing Company, Inc. These publications on proven management techniques for small businesses are available from Upstart Publishing Company, Inc., 12 Portland Street, Dover, NH 03820. For a free current catalog, call 800-235-8866 outside New Hampshire, or 749-5071 in state.

- ***The Business Planning Guide***, 1992, David H. Bangs, Jr. and Upstart Publishing Company, Inc. A manual that helps you write a business plan and financing proposal tailored to your business, your goals and your resources. Includes worksheets and checklists. (Softcover, 208 pages, $19.95)

- ***The Market Planning Guide***, 1990, David H. Bangs, Jr. and Upstart Publishing Company, Inc. A manual to help small-business owners put together a goal-oriented, resource-based marketing plan with action steps, benchmarks and time lines. Includes worksheets and checklists to make implementation and review easier. (Softcover, 160 pages, $19.95)

- **The Cash Flow Control Guide**, 1990, David H. Bangs, Jr. and Upstart Publishing Company, Inc. A manual to help small-business owners solve their number-one financial problem. Includes worksheets and checklists. (Softcover, 88 pages, $14.95)

- **The Personnel Planning Guide**, 1988, David H. Bangs, Jr. and Upstart Publishing Company, Inc. A 176-page manual outlining practical, proven personnel management techniques, including hiring, managing, evaluating and compensating personnel. Includes worksheets and checklists. (Softcover, 176 pages, $19.95)

- **The Start Up Guide: A One-Year Plan for Entrepreneurs**, 1989, David H. Bangs, Jr. and Upstart Publishing Company, Inc. This book utilizes the same step-by-step, no-jargon method as the *Business Planning Guide*, to help even those with no business training through the process of beginning a successful business. (Softcover, 160 pages, $19.95)

- **Managing by the Numbers: Financial Essentials for the Growing Business**, 1992, David H. Bangs, Jr. and Upstart Publishing Company, Inc. Straightforward techniques for getting the maximum return with a minimum of detail in your business's financial management. (Softcover, 160 pages, $19.95)

- **On Your Own: A Woman's Guide to Building a Business**, 1990, Laurie Zuckerman, Upstart Publishing Company, Inc. *On Your Own* is for women who want hands-on, practical information about starting and running a business. It deals honestly with issues like finding time for your business when you're also the primary care provider, societal biases against women and credit discrimination. (Softcover, 224 pages, $18.95)

- **Buy the Right Business—At the Right Price**, 1990, Brian Knight and the Associates of Country Business, Inc., Upstart Publishing Company, Inc. Many people who would like to be in business for themselves think strictly of starting a business. In some cases, buying a going concern may be preferable—and just as affordable. (Softcover, 152 pages, $18.95)

- **Borrowing for Your Business**, 1991, George M. Dawson, Upstart Publishing Company, Inc. This is a book for borrowers and about lenders. Includes detailed guidelines on selecting a bank and a banker, answering the lender's seven most important questions, how your banker looks at a loan and how to get a loan renewed. (Hardcover, 160 pages, $19.95)

- **Problem Employees**, 1991, Dr. Peter Wylie and Dr. Mardy Grothe, Upstart Publishing Company, Inc. Provides managers and supervisors with a simple, practical and straightforward approach to help all employees, especially problem employees, significantly improve their work performance. (Softcover, 272 pages, $22.95)

- **Marketing Sourcebook for Small Business**, 1989, Jeffrey P. Davidson, John Wylie Publishing. A good introductory book for small business owners with excellent definitions of important marketing terms and concepts. (Hardcover, 325 pages, $24.95)

- **Guerrilla Marketing: Secrets for Making Big Profits from Your Small Business,** 1984, J. Conrad Levinson, Houghton-Mifflin. A classic tool kit for small businesses. (Hardcover, 226 pages, $14.95)

- **Forecasting Sales and Planning Profits: A No Nonsense Guide for a Growing Business**, 1986, Kenneth E. Marino, Probus Publishing Co. Concise and easily applied forecasting system based on an analysis of market potential and sale requirements, which helps establish the basis for financial statements in your business plan. (Hardcover, 177 pages)

Periodicals

Small Business Reporter. An excellent series of booklets on small business management published by Bank of America, Department 3120, PO Box 37000, San Francisco, CA 94137 (415) 622-2491. Individual copies are $5 each. Ask for a list of current titles—they have about 17 available, including *Steps to Starting a Business, Avoiding Management Pitfalls, Business Financing* and *Marketing Small Business.*

In Business. A bimonthly magazine for small businesses, especially those with less than 10 employees. The publisher is J.G. Press, PO Box 323, Emmaus, PA 18049. Annual subscriptions are $18.

Inc. One of the leading small business magazines. 38 Commercial Wharf, Boston, MA 02110 (617) 248-8000.

D & B Reports. Excellent case studies and updated financial information for small businesses. Dun and Bradstreet, 299 Park Ave., New York, NY 10171 (212) 593-6724.

Small Business Forum: Journal of the Association of Small Business Development Centers. Case studies and analyses of small-business problems gleaned from a nationwide network of small-business development professionals. Includes book reviews. Reprints available. Issued three times a year, $25.00 per year. University of Wisconsin, SBDC, 432 North Wake St., Madison, WI 53706.

Appendices

Other Tools for Small-Business Owners

Software for small businesses. We recommend fisCAL™, a product of the Halcyon Group, 449 Fleming Rd., Charleston, SC 29412 (803) 795-7336. fisCAL™ and its accompanying manual, *Profit from Financial Statements*, provide a sophisticated financial analysis system for most small businesses. fisCAL™ includes updated financial data from the Robert Morris Associates (RMA) Annual Statement Studies, Financial Research Associates', Financial Statement Studies of the Small Business Annual and Halcyon's Financial Profiles of the Small Business.

Financial Templates. PSI Research 300 N. Valley Drive, Grants Pass, OR 97526 offers excellent financial templates for small-business owners. Small Business Expert is for use with IBM and compatibles and Financial Templates for Small Business is for use with Excel™ on the Macintosh™. You may also find ready-made templates for specific business applications available from local computer clubs.

Additional Resources

Small Business Development Centers (SBDCs). Call your state university or the Small Business Administration (SBA) to find the SBDC nearest you. Far and away the best free management program available, SBDCs provide expert assistance and training in every aspect of business management. Don't ignore this resource.

SCORE, or Service Corps of Retired Executives. Sponsored by the U.S. Small Business Administration, provides free counseling and also a series of workshops and seminars for small businesses. Of special interest: SCORE offers a Business Planning Workshop, which includes a 30-minute video produced specifically for SCORE by Upstart Publishing and funded by Paychex, Inc. There are over 500 SCORE chapters nationwide. For more information, contact the SBA office nearest you and ask about SCORE.

Small Business Administration (SBA). The SBA offers a number of management assistance programs. If you are assigned a capable Management Assistance Officer, you have an excellent resource. The SBA is worth a visit, if only to leaf through their extensive literature.

Colleges and universities. Most have business courses. Some have SBDCs, others have more specialized programs. Some have small-business expertise—the University of New Hampshire, for example, has two schools that provide direct small-business management assistance.

Keye Productivity Center, P.O. Box 23192, Kansas City, MO 64141. Keye Productivity offers business seminars on specific personnel topics for a reasonable fee. Call them at (800) 821-3919 for topics and prices. Their seminar entitled Hiring and Firing is excellent, well-documented and useful. Good handout materials are included.

Comprehensive Accounting Corporation, 2111 Comprehensive Drive, Aurora, IL 60507. CAC has over 425 franchised offices providing accounting, bookkeeping and management consulting services to small businesses. For information, call (800) 323-9009.

Center for Entrepreneurial Management, 29 Greene Street, New York, NY 10013. The oldest and largest nonprofit membership association for small-business owners in the world. They maintain an extensive list of books, videotapes, cassettes and other small-business management aids. Call (212) 925-7304 for information.

Libraries. Do not forget to take advantage of the information readily available at your local library.

Appendix Four: Glossary

"Acid Test" Ratio: Cash, plus other assets that can be immediately converted to cash, should equal or exceed current liabilities. The formula used to determine the ratio is as follows:
Cash plus Receivables (net) +
Marketable Securities =
Current Liabilities
The "acid test" ratio is one of the most important credit barometers used by lending institutions, as it indicates the ability of a business enterprise to meet its current obligations.

Aging Receivables: A scheduling of accounts receivable according to the length of time they have been outstanding. This shows which accounts are not being paid in a timely manner and may reveal any difficulty in collecting long-overdue receivables. This may also be an important indicator of developing cash flow problems.

Amortization: To liquidate on an installment basis; the process of gradually paying off a liability over a period of time, i.e., a mortgage is amortized by periodically paying off part of the face amount of the mortgage.

Assets: The valuable resources, or properties and property rights owned by an individual or business enterprise.

Balance Sheet: An itemized statement that lists the total assets, liabilities, and net worth of a given business to reflect its financial condition at a given moment in time.

Beverage Cost or Beverage Cost Percentage: refers to the cost of the ingredients in a beverage expressed as a percentage of the selling price.

Capital: Capital funds are those funds that are needed for the base of the business. Usually they are put into the business in a fairly permanent form such as in fixed assets, plant and equipment, or are used in other ways that are not recoverable in the short run unless the entire business is sold.

Capital Equipment: Equipment used to manufacture a product, provide a service, or to sell, store, and deliver merchandise. Such equipment will not be sold in the normal course of business, but will be used and worn out or be consumed over time as business is conducted.

Cash Flow: The actual movement of cash within a business: cash inflow minus cash outflow. A term used to designate the reported net income of a corporation plus amounts charged off for depreciation, depletion, amortization, and extraordinary charges to reserves, which are bookkeeping deductions and not actually paid out in cash. Used to offer a better indication of the ability of a firm to meet its own obligations and to pay dividends, rather than the conventional net income figure.

Cash Position: See Liquidity.

Collateral: An asset pledged to a lender in order to support the loan.

Covers: The number of meals served in a given period of time. A restaurant that serves 120 lunches would be described as serving 120 covers at lunch.

Current Assets: Cash or other items that will normally be turned into cash within one year, and assets that will be used up in the operations of a firm within one year.

Current Liabilities: Amounts owed that will ordinarily be paid by a firm within one year. Such items include accounts payable, wages payable, taxes payable, the current portion of a long-term debt, and interest and dividends payable.

Current Ratio: A ratio of a firm's current assets to its current liabilities. Because a current ratio includes the value of inventories that have not yet been sold, it does not offer the best evaluation of the firm's current status. The "acid test" ratio, covering the most liquid of current assets, produces a better evaluation.

Debt: Debt refers to borrowed funds, whether from your own coffers or from other individuals, banks or institutions. It is generally secured with a note, which in turn may be secured by a lien against property or other assets. Ordinarily, the note states repayment and interest provisions, which vary greatly in both amount and duration, depending upon the purpose, source and terms of the loan. Some debt is convertible, that is, it may be changed into direct ownership of a portion of a business under certain stated conditions.

Demographics: (1) The statistical study of human populations, especially with reference to size and density, distribution and vital statistics.

Demographics: (2) Relating to the dynamic balance of a population, especially with regard to density and capacity for expansion or decline.

Demographic Segmentation: A marketing analysis that targets groups of prospects by factors such as sex, age, marital status, income, occupation, family size, and education (from *Forecasting Sales and Planning Profits*, Kenneth E. Marino).

Distribution: The delivery or conveyance of a good or service to a market.

Distribution Channel: The chain of intermediaries linking the producer of a good to the consumer.

Equity: Equity is the owner's investment in the business. Unlike capital, equity is what remains after the liabilities of the company are subtracted from the assets—thus it may be greater than or less than the capital invested in the business. Equity investment carries with it a share of ownership and usually a share in profits, as well as some say in how the business is managed.

Food Cost or Food Cost Percentage: refers to the cost of the raw food ingredients of an item expressed as a percentage of the selling price.

Gross Profit: Net sales (sales minus returned merchandise, discounts, or other allowances) minus the cost of goods sold.

Guaranty: A pledge by a third party to repay a loan in the event that the borrower cannot.

Income Statement: A statement of income and expenses for a given period of time.

Inventory: The materials owned and held by a business firm, including new materials, intermediate products and parts, work-in-process and finished goods, intended either for internal consumption or for sale.

Liquidity: A term used to describe the solvency of a business, and which has special reference to the degree of readiness in which assets can be converted into cash without a loss. Also called Cash Position. If a firm's current assets cannot be converted into cash to meet current liabilities, the firm is said to be Illiquid.

Loan Agreement: A document that states what a business can or cannot do as long as it owes money to (usually) a bank. A loan agreement may place restrictions on the owner's salary, on dividends, on the amount of other debt, on working capital limits, on sales, or on the number of additional personnel.

Loans: Debt money for private business is usually in the form of bank loans, which, in a sense, are personal because a private business can be harder to evaluate in terms of creditworthiness and degree of risk. A secured loan is a loan that is backed up by a claim against some asset or assets of a business. An unsecured loan is backed by the faith the bank has in the borrower's ability to pay back the money.

Long-Term Liabilities: These are liabilities (expenses) that will not mature within the next year.

Net Worth: The owner's equity in a given business represented by the excess of the total assets over the total amounts owed to outside creditors (total liabilities) at a given moment in time. Also, the net worth of an individual as determined by deducting the amount of all his or her personal liabilities from the total value of personal assets. Generally refers to tangible net worth, which does not include goodwill, etc.

Note: The basic business loan, a note represents a loan that will be repaid, or substantially reduced 30, 60, or 90 days later at a stated interest rate. These are short-term, and unless they are made under a line of credit, a separate loan application is needed for each loan and each renewal.

Partnership: A legal relationship created by the voluntary association of two or more persons to carry on as co-owners of a business for profit; a type of business organization in which two or more persons agree on the amount of their contributions (capital and effort) and on the distribution of profits, if any.

Positioning: A marketing method based on determining what market niche your business should fill, and how it should promote its products or services in light of competitive and other forces.

Pro Forma: A projection or an estimate of what may result in the future from actions in the present. A *pro forma* financial statement is one that shows how the actual operations of a business will turn out if certain assumptions are realized.

Profit: The excess of the selling price over all costs and expenses incurred in making a sale. Also, the reward to the entrepreneur for the risks assumed by him or her in the establishment, operations, and management of a given enterprise or undertaking.

Sole Proprietorship or Proprietorship: A type of business organization in which one individual owns the business. Legally, the owner is the business and personal assets are typically exposed to liabilities of the business.

Sub-Chapter S Corporation or Tax Option Corporation: A corporation that has elected under Sub-Chapter S of the IRS Tax Code (by unanimous consent of its shareholders) not to pay any corporate tax on its income and, instead, to have the shareholders pay taxes on it, even though it is not distributed. Shareholders of a tax option corporation are also entitled to deduct, on their individual returns, their shares of any net operating loss sustained by the corporation, subject to limitations in the tax code. In many respects, Sub-Chapter S permits a corporation to behave for tax purposes as a proprietorship or partnership.

Takeover: The acquisition of one company by another company.

Target Market: The specific individuals, distinguished by socio-economic, demographic, and/or interest characteristics, who are the most likely potential customers for the goods and/or services of a business.

Term Loans: Either secured or unsecured, usually for periods of more than a year to as many as ten. Term loans are paid off like a mortgage: so many dollars per month for so many years. The most common uses of term loans are for equipment and other fixed assets, for working capital, and for real estate.

Turns: (or turnover) refers to the number of times every seat in the restaurant was used during a given meal period. A restaurant with 100 seats that served 120 lunches would be described as doing 1.2 turns for lunch.

Working Capital: The difference between current assets and current liabilities. Contrasted with capital, which is a permanent use of funds, working capital cycles through your business in a variety of forms: inventories, accounts and notes receivable, and cash and securities.

Appendix Five: Worksheets

These blank worksheets and forms are for you to fill out and use.

Your Restaurant
Computation of Selling Price and
Food Cost Percentage by Menu Item

Food Item	"Q" A	Other Food B	Total Raw Food Cost $ C	Suggested Selling Price at X% Food Cost D	Actual Selling Price E	Food Cost % (C/E)x100

A   Compute the raw food cost of "Q" or all the food items included in the price of the meal except for the main item. Included in the "Q" should be salad, starch, bread and butter, garnishes, and anything else that is included with the price of the entree.

B   Compute the raw food cost of the entree.

C   Add columns A + B.

D   Divide column C by the desired food cost percentage. For example, if you desire a 35% food cost, divide by 0.35.

E   Adjust the actual selling price up or down depending upon other factors such as perceived value, high labor cost for that item, competitive prices in the market, etc.

F   Compute the projected food cost percentage by dividing column C by column E and multiplying by 100 for a percentage.

Your Restaurant
Projected Income Statement—By Month, Jan. 1 to Dec. 31, 19___

	JAN	FEB	MAR	APR	MAY	JUN	JUL	AUG	SEPT	OCT	NOV	DEC	TOTALS	%
Sales														
Food														
Beverage														
Total Sales														
Cost of Sales														
Food														
Beverage														
Total Cost of Sales														
Gross Profit														
Other Income														
Total Income														
Controllable Expenses														
Payroll														
Employee Benefits														
Direct Operating Exp.														
Advertising & Promotion														
Utilities														
Administrative & General														
Repairs & Maintenance														
Total Controllable Exp.														
Income Before Occupancy Costs														
Occupancy Costs														
Rent														
Property Taxes														
Other Taxes														
Property Insurance														
Total Occupancy Costs														
Income Before Interest and Dep.														
Interest														
Depreciation														
Restaurant Profit														
Other Deductions														
Income Before Income Taxes														

Your Restaurant
Income Projection—By Quarter
Year 19____

	1st Quarter	2nd Quarter	3rd Quarter	4th Quarter	Total	Percent
Sales						
Food						
Beverage						
Total Sales						
Cost of Sales						
Food						
Beverage						
Total Cost of Sales						
Gross Profit						
Other Income						
Total Income						
Controllable Expenses						
Payroll						
Employee Benefits						
Direct Operating Exp.						
Advertising & Promotion						
Utilities						
Administrative & General						
Repairs & Maintenance						
Total Controllable Exp.						
Income Before Occupancy Costs						
Occupancy Costs						
Rent						
Property Taxes						
Other Taxes						
Property Insurance						
Total Occupancy Costs						
Income Before Interest and Dep.						
Interest						
Depreciation						
Restaurant Profit						
Other Deductions						
Income Before Income Taxes						

Your Restaurant
Cash Flow Projections—By Month
Year____, Jan. 1 to Dec. 31, 19___

	JAN	FEB	MAR	APR	MAY	JUN	JUL	AUG	SEPT	OCT	NOV	DEC	TOTALS
Cash Receipts													
Food Sales													
Beverage Sales													
Sales Receivables													
Other Income													
Total Cash Receipts													
Cash Disbursements													
Cost of Sales, Food													
Cost of Sales, Beverages													
Controllable Expenses													
Payroll													
Employee Benefits													
Direct Operating Exp.													
Advertising & Promotion													
Utilities													
Administrative & General													
Repairs & Maintenance													
Occupancy Costs													
Rent													
Property Taxes													
Other Taxes													
Property Insurance													
Interest													
Other Deductions													
Total Cash Disbursements:													

Appendices

Cash Flow From Operations																				
Cash Receipts																				
Less: Cash Disbursements																				
Net From Operations																				
Cash on Hand																				
Opening Balance																				
Plus: New Loan (Debt)																				
Plus: New Investment																				
Plus: Sale of Fixed Assets																				
Plus: Net From Operations																				
Total Cash Available																				
Less: Debt Reduction																				
Less: New Fixed Assets																				
Less: Dividends to Stockholders																				
Less: Stock Redemption																				
Less: Loans to Officers																				
Total Cash Paid Out																				
Cash Position—Ending Balance																				

Appendices

Your Restaurant
Cash Flow Projections—By Quarter, Year_____

	1st Quarter	2nd Quarter	3rd Quarter	4th Quarter	Total
Cash Receipts					
Food Sales					
Beverage Sales					
Sales Receivables					
Other Income					
Total Cash Receipts					
Cash Disbursements					
Cost of Sales, Food					
Cost of Sales, Beverages					
Controllable Expenses					
Payroll					
Employee Benefits					
Direct Operating Exp.					
Advertising & Promotion					
Utilities					
Administrative & General					
Repairs & Maintenance					
Occupancy Costs					
Rent					
Property Taxes					
Other Taxes					
Property Insurance					
Interest					
Other Deductions					
Total Cash Disbursements:					
Cash Flow From Operations					
Cash Receipts					
Less: Cash Disbursements					
Net From Operations					
Cash on Hand					
Opening Balance					
Plus: New Loan (Debt)					
Plus: New Investment					
Plus: Sale of Fixed Assets					
Plus: Net From Operations					
Total Cash Available					
Less: Debt Reduction					
Less: New Fixed Assets					
Less: Dividends to Stockholders					
Less: Stock Redemption					
Less: Loans to Officers					
Total Cash Paid Out					
Cash Position—Ending Balance					

Personal Data Sheet

Name _____ Date of birth _____

Address _____

Telephone number _____ Years there _____

Marital status _____ Name of spouse _____ Dependents _____

Education

	Name and address	Grades completed/ diplomas/degrees obtained
High School		
Other		

Military service _____ Years _____

Highest rank obtained _____

Relevant training or work experience _____

_____

Work Experience

Business and Address	Job title and duties	Supervisor	Dates

Trade, professional or civic membership and activities _____

_____

Hobbies, interests, other relevant information _____

_____

Use another sheet if necessary.

Credit Inquiry

Name _____ Date of birth _____

Address _____

Telephone number _____ Years there _____

Former Address _____

_____ Years there _____

Marital Status _____ Name of Spouse _____ No. dependents _____

Employer _____ Years there _____

Address _____

Phone _____ Kind of business _____

Position _____ Net income $/_____

Former employer and address _____ Years there _____

Spouse's employer and address _____

Net income $/_____ Other income sources: $/month _____

Account	Bank	Acct. No.	Balance
Checking			
Savings			

Auto owned (year and make) _____ Purchased from _____ $ _____

Financed by _____ Balance owed $ _____ Monthly _____

Rent or mortgage payment/mo. $ _____ Paid to _____

Real estate owned in name of _____ Purchase price _____ Mtge. bal. __

Credit references and all debts owed—other than above
(Bank, loan or finance cos., credit unions, budget)

Name	Address	Orig. amt.	Bal.	Mo. payment

Life insurance amount _____ Company _____

If co-maker for others, state where and for whom _____

Nearest relative or friend not living with you/relationship _____

Address _____

Appendices

Cost of Living Budget

(Based on average month—does not cover purchase of any new items except emergency replacements.)

Detailed Budget

Regular Monthly Payments

House payments (principal, interest, taxes, insurance) or rent	$ _____
Car payments (including insurance)	$ _____
Appliance, TV payments	$ _____
Home improvement loan payments	$ _____
Personal loan, credit card payments	$ _____
Health plan payments	$ _____
Life insurance premiums	$ _____
Other insurance premiums	$ _____
Savings/investments	$ _____
Total	$ _____

Household Operating Expense

Telephone	$ _____
Gas and electricity	$ _____
Water	$ _____
Other household expenses, repairs, maintenance	$ _____
Total	$ _____

Personal Expense

Clothing, cleaning, laundry	$ _____
Prescription medications	$ _____
Physicians, dentists	$ _____
Education	$ _____
Dues	$ _____
Gifts and contributions	$ _____

(Continued)

Travel .... $ _____

Newspapers, magazines, books .... $ _____

Auto upkeep and gas .... $ _____

Spending money and allowances .... $ _____

Miscellaneous .... $ _____

Total .... $ _____

Food Expense

Food—at home .... $ _____

Food—away from home .... $ _____

Total .... $ _____

Tax Expense

Federal and state income taxes .... $ _____

Other taxes not included above .... $ _____

Total .... $ _____

Budget Summary

A. Income gross

    Monthly total .... $ _____

Less expense:

Regular monthly payments .... $ _____

Household operating expense .... $ _____

Personal expense .... $ _____

Food expense .... $ _____

Tax expense .... $ _____

Monthly total .... $ _____

B. Monthly total expenses .... $ _____

Savings (A – B) .... $ _____

Appendices

Cost of Living Budget

(Based on average month—does not cover purchase of any new items except emergency replacements.)

Detailed Budget

Regular Monthly Payments

House payments
(principal, interest, taxes, insurance) or rent .... $ _____

Car payments (including insurance) .... $ _____

Appliance, TV payments .... $ _____

Home improvement loan payments .... $ _____

Personal loan, credit card payments .... $ _____

Health plan payments .... $ _____

Life insurance premiums .... $ _____

Other insurance premiums .... $ _____

Savings/investments .... $ _____

Total .... $ _____

Household Operating Expense

Telephone .... $ _____

Gas and electricity .... $ _____

Water .... $ _____

Other household expenses, repairs, maintenance .... $ _____

Total .... $ _____

Personal Expense

Clothing, cleaning, laundry .... $ _____

Prescription medications .... $ _____

Physicians, dentists .... $ _____

Education .... $ _____

Dues .... $ _____

Gifts and contributions .... $ _____

(Continued)

Travel .... $ _____

Newspapers, magazines, books .... $ _____

Auto upkeep and gas .... $ _____

Spending money and allowances .... $ _____

Miscellaneous .... $ _____

Total .... $ _____

Food Expense

Food—at home .... $ _____

Food—away from home .... $ _____

Total .... $ _____

Tax Expense

Federal and state income taxes .... $ _____

Other taxes not included above .... $ _____

Total .... $ _____

Budget Summary

A. Income gross

    Monthly total .... $ _____

Less expense:

Regular monthly payments .... $ _____

Household operating expense .... $ _____

Personal expense .... $ _____

Food expense .... $ _____

Tax expense .... $ _____

Monthly total .... $ _____

B. Monthly total expenses .... $ _____

Savings (A – B) .... $ _____

Index

Accounting system, 55
Acid test ratio, 65; defined, 131
Acquisition. *See* Takeover
Advertising, budget, 34
Amortization, defined, 131
Application of funds statement, 90-91
Assets, current, 62, 132; fixed, 63, 131

Balance sheet, 63-66; defined 131
Bank financing, kinds of, 109-111. *See also* Financing
Bookkeeping system, set up. 55-58
Break-even analysis, 67-70
Budget deviation analysis. *See* Deviation analysis
Business plan, and financing proposal, 105; main parts of, 18; new restaurant, 11; outline of, 2; takeover, 12

Capital, defined, 131; equipment list, 60-61
Cash flow, defined, 132; projection, 81-90; management, 83
Cash position. *See* Liquidity
Collateral, defined, 132
Competition, 23-24, 37-39
Corporate checklist, sample, 121-122
Covers, defined, 132
Credit, customer, 23; line of, 110; three Cs of,107; trade, 12
Current ratio, 65; defined 132

Debt, defined, 7; equity vs., 106-109; intermediate, 109; long-term and short-term, 109-111. *See also* Financing
Demographic Segmentation, 19-20, defined 132
Depreciation, 60, 63
Description of business, 9-14
Deviation analysis, 92-97
Distribution, defined, 133

Equity, defined, 133; funds, 7

Financial reports, historical, 101
Financing, 7; application and effect of loan, 48-50; intermediate, 109-110; long-term, 109-110; proposal, 105; short-term, 109-110
Fixed Costs, 67
Food cost, overall computation of, 32; percentage, 28-29. *See also* Pricing strategy
Funding, sources and application of, 59

Glossary, 131-135
Gross profit, 74; computation of, 31
Guaranty, defined, 133

Income, projections, 71-80; statement format, 72-74
Inventory, defined, 133
Investor, equity, 7

Letters, sample, 114-115
Liabilities, current, 63, 132; long-term, 63, 132
Line of credit, revolving and nonrevolving, 110
Liquidity, defined, 133; and profitability, 57-58
Loan agreement, defined, 133
Loans, 7; application and expected effect of, 48-50; defined, 133; secured and unsecured, 109; term, defined, 134
Location of business, 35-36

Management, 40-44
Market niche, 24
Marketing, 17-34; sample description, 34

Net worth, 63
Note, defined, 134

Partnership, agreement sample, 117-121; defined, 134
Personnel, 45-47
Positioning, 24-26; defined, 134
Pricing strategy, 27-29
Pro forma, 71; defined, 134
Profit, defined, 134
Profit and loss statement. *See* Income
Projected income statement, 71-80
Promotion, 24-26; pyramid, 25
Proprietorship, defined, 134
Publicity, 24-26

Quick ratio, 65

Ratio analysis, 65
Resources for restaurateurs, 125-130
Résumés, functional, 123; sample, 113

Sales forecasts, 75
Selling price, computation of, 28-29
Small business, available resources, 43-44
Sole proprietorship, defined, 134
Spreadsheets, as control documents, 56-58; software programs, 82
Sub-Chapter S corporation, defined, 134
Supporting documents, 113-116

Takeover, defined, 134
Target markets, 19, 24; defined, 134
Tax option corporation. *See* Sub-Chapter S corporation
Trade credit, 12
Turns, 70; defined, 135

Index

Uniform System of Accounts for Restaurants: income statement format, 73; principal benefits, 55

Variable costs, 67

Working capital, calculating, 65; defined 135
Worksheets, blank, 137-156